The Politics of Hope (After the War)

The Politics of Hope (After the War)
Selected and New Poems

Dubravka Djurić

Foreword by Charles Bernstein

**Edited and translated with an interview
by Biljana D. Obradović**

ROOF BOOKS
New York

ISBN: 978-0-937804-94-0
Library of Congress Control Number: 2023948304

Cover: Still frame from Dubravka Djurić's video work from early 1980s.
Cover design by Deborah Thomas.
Author photo © 2023 Miško Šuvaković.

Republic of Serbia
Ministry of Culture

The translations in this selection of poems have been made possible by a generous grant from the Ministry of Culture and Information of the Republic of Serbia.

This book is made possible, in part, by the New York State Council on the Arts with the support of the Office of the Governor and the New York State Legislature.

Roof Books
are published by
Segue Foundation
300 Bowery, New York, NY 10012
seguefoundation.com

Roof Books
are distributed by
Small Press Distribution
1341 Seventh Street
Berkeley, CA. 94710-1403
800-869-7553 or spdbooks.org

for Miško Šuvaković

Table of Contents

Thanks

Dubravka Djurić wishes to thank Biljana Obradović for deciding to do this work and for the exciting interaction during the translating process. She also thanks Nataša Teofilović, graphic designer, Darija Žilić, and Aleksandra Izgarjan. Thanks to Charles Bernstein and Susan Bee. Thanks to Marjorie Perloff and Juliana Spahr. Dubravka would like to stress the importance of the three collectives to her work: Community for Space Research, *ProFemina*, and AWIN School of Poetry and Theory. Special thanks to Miško Šuvaković for his unconditional lifetime support.

Biljana Obradović wishes to thank Dubravka Djurić for the confidence in letting me translate these poems, and all the help given throughout the process, and to Charles Bernstein for introducing Dubravka to Biljana and for writing the foreword. She wishes to thank Xavier University of Louisiana's Provost, Dr. Anne McCall, and the Head of the Department of English, Dr. Oliver Hennessey, for the Spring 2021 sabbatical leave so that she could work on this project. She also wishes to thank those who always help her with the process of translation, especially Elizabeta Ivović Holt and John Gery; and for moral support, as always, Vesna Kilibarda. She also wishes to thank her son, Petar Gery, and her husband, John Gery, for all their support.

Foreword

Go Tell Aunt Rhody: Dubravka's Djurić's Courage

In post-communist society, which shows an unambiguous tendency towards the totalitarian model of life, writing and editing should have the goal of protecting the necessity of pluralism, multiculturalism, and difference in life and culture.
—Dubravka Djurić, "A Few Statements on Politics and Power in Culture" (2001)[1]

Then I came to the questions of identity and of language, which have occupied me since 1991. The decomposition of one socialist multi-cultural country imposes the demand for redefining one's identity. The identity matrix was changing in a brutal way, and you have to decide and choose between newly established matrices for identification.
—Djurić, "I Wonna Talk to You" (2011)[2]

Go tell Aunt Rhody
Go tell Aunt Rhody
Go tell Aunt Rhody
The old gray goose is dead
— Traditional (American)

The Politics of Hope (After the War) is an act of defiance and delight: both a refusal to be caught in the "traps" that are the given state of things, aesthetically or politically, but also an insistence on the pleasure of possibilities. Djurić's poetry is both performative and conceptual. *Conceptual* in the sense of cosmogonic: it's as if the cosmos is constantly coming into being in the here and now of the poems. This is not immaculate conception but the muddy kind. Djurić knows that for poetry to hit pay dirt, it must be close to the ground, where *here* is *heard*.

---

[1] Djurić EPC page: <writing.upenn.edu/library/Djuric-Dubravka_poems.html>. See also, on this page, links to Djurić on Slobodan Tišma and Vasko Popa. "Experimental Poetry in Yugoslav and Post-Yugoslav Literary Spaces: Socialism, War Transition and Beyond" is forthcoming in *boundary 2*.

[2] <sibila.com.br/english/i-wonna-talk-to-you/9679>.

Dubravka Djurić and I have been in conversation for over thirty years, mostly in letters but also in Buffalo and Manhattan, Belgrade and Novi Sad, Budapest and Pécs. We've worked together on translations, books, anthologies, magazines, essays, readings, and poems.[3] While our exchanges are in English, the language we speak to each other is less invested in nation states or given identities than what Robin Blaser called "image nation": an imaginary in-between that commands our first loyalty. And Dubravka has been my guide to the astonishing poetry, poetics, and art of the former Yugoslavia, from the dazzling, 600 pages of *Impossible Histories: Historic Avant-Gardes, Neo-Avant-Gardes, and Post-Avant-Gardes in Yugoslavia, 1918–1991*, edited by Djurić with Miško Šuvaković (MIT Press, 2003) and *Cat Painters: An Anthology of Contemporary Serbian Poetry*, edited by Biljana D. Obradović, with Djurić, for which I wrote a foreword (Diálogos, 2016).

I first met Dubravka, along with Miško, in the summer of 1991 in Beograd, in the company of James Sherry, publisher of this book. Dubravka and I had been in correspondence since the Fall of 1989, when she wrote me about translating poems and doing an interview for an issue of *Polja* and poems and poetics for *Delo*. Since James and I were to be in Vienna for a reading at Alte Schmeide, I proposed to Dubravka that we visit her. I figured it was just 400 miles, about the same distance to my new job in Buffalo from my home in New York City. But that only goes to show how little *same* can mean. In Vienna, we rented a (goddamn small) car and headed for Belgrade. We had only enough time to stay one night in Budapest. That next day, when we got to the Yugoslavian border, we felt an implosive darkness, intimations of impending war. In Bel-grade, the streets were filled with clusters of young men looking for a fight they would soon get. I have no idea how we found Dubravka's and Miško's house, since directions have never been my forte and the street signs were in a foreign alphabet. But we managed. It was an old house with a yard, on a back street, which Dubravka and Miško shared with Miško's parents. The grounds were very close to the football stadium; on game days you could hear the roar of the crowd.

The minute we were with Dubravka and Miško that outside roar subsided; everything changed, my anxiety lifted. Theirs was a world of artists, intellect-tuals, feminists, and anti-nationalist activists. They were eager to introduce us

---

[3] For example, *Teške pesme* [Difficult Poems] by Čarls Bernstin [selected poems], ed. & tr. Dubravka Djurić (Montenegro: d.o.o. OKF Cetinje), 2016.

to friends in Beograd and Novi Sad. Our connection to each other was quick and indelible. I felt an artistic and personal comradery with them: *gemütlich*.

Just before we left Belgrade, after several enthralling days of conversation and readings, Dubravka gave me two bottles of spirits, farm-made *rakija*, since I had been drinking this throughout the visit, being an aficionado of local liquor (it calms my nerves). One of those bottles slipped through my hands and shattered on the driveway. Go figure.

A few years later, Dubravka and Miško came for a one-month residency at the Buffalo Poetics Program. Dubravka had a front row seat to what we were creating and that deepened our connection, our sense of a shared poetics/aesthetics/politics.

A few years later, during the NATO bombing of Belgrade, Dubravka and I emailed frequently–we were on neither side and that *neither* became our shared homeland. Dubravka published her letters in *Chain* with the title "Letter from Belgrade" (1999). I continued that dialog in an improvised poem at the Whitney Museum, "Talk to Me," which was collected in *Recalculating*. Dubravka, in turn, published a response, which she called, "I Wonna Talk to You."[4]

All poetry is local despite the frequent obscenity of high- and middle-minded humanists that great poetry is universal and timeless, as if there was a one-size-fits-all verse for a unified world, as if poetry wasn't flooded by time. Djurić's poems thicken when read within (and against) the context of her time and place: some basic history helps (of Yugoslavia and the Cold War and of "post-Communism" in Serbia) as well as some sense of the postwar poetry and art in Serbia, Croatia, Bosnia, Montenegro, and Slovenia, in particular. Fortunately, *Cat Painters* and *Impossible Histories* offer introductions.[5]

---

[4] "Letter from Belgrade" and "I Wonna Talk to You" are linked at Djurić's EPC page, cited above. *Chain* was edited by Jena Osman and Juliana Spahr, who were Poetics Program graduate students at the time of Djurić's visit. Djurić contributed to the first issue of *Chain* in 1994, which focused on gender and editing; she also contributed "Identiteti" to the fifth issue on "Different Languages" (1998). See also Djurić's PennSound page, including our 2019 Close Listening conversation and a recording I made of her poetry in 2007: <writing.upenn.edu/pennsound/x/Djuric.php>.

[5] See also "Experimental Poetry in Yugoslav and Post-Yugoslav Literary Spaces: Socialism, War, Transition and Beyond," *boundary 2*, 2023.

Biljana D. Obradović shows ingenuity and verve in bringing these poems into English.

All poetry is local but is riven by the exogamic. Djurić's has one parent from Serbia and another from Croatia; she says her mother tongue is "Serbo-Croatian"—a language that no longer officially exists. Exogamic means marrying outside your group; for poetry it means trafficking in contradictory styles: a refusal of a single lyric identity (or a single identity of a poem). Djurić's work means to break the hold of nationalism and linearity through miscegenated forms and multiplanar approaches to nonconventional narrative. "To control means to IMPOVERISH," she writes.

It's not that conventional lyric is too poetic, but that it's not poetic enough.

"A poem writes itself in the rhythm of movement." Djurić's exogamic practice moves from conceptual to visual/concrete to bricolage to poetics to dazzlingly looping prose (as in the powerful "Rule of Emptiness [After the War]"). These poems channel and challenge self-reflectivity: "A Non-Narrative Poem of Poetry" is addressed to the poem being written. At times Djurić's work takes a polemic and theatrical turn: these explicitly feminist poems have a dense exuberance that refuses to be corralled. You want accessible poems?, she seems to ask in one poem. Well, she answers sardonically, porn is accessible. In this way, Djurić links the porn created by the objectification of a woman's body with the aesthetic porn created by the objectification of emotion or sentiment in the service of official nationalist (or socialist) verse. Djurić's disjunction allows for a new version of realism and a reimagination of the possibilities for political poetry.

But if the poems prize disruption, Djurić holds to her motto, "No disrupt-tion is absolute." Because, she wryly notes, "The closest exit is a blind alley." There is no retreat into the asemic in these works: sense is at stake. Nor is there refuge in nostalgia: Nostalgia, she writes in a footnote, is "a café in the center of Ljubljana."

Courage is hard to come by and in poetry even rarer than the nectar of justice. I don't mean bravado, that's plentiful and often necessary, depending on which side of history you land on (yes, I know I've said that in Djurić's poetry history doesn't have sides). Courage in poetry is grounded in what Hölderlin calls timidity (*Blödigkeit*): the ability not to know, not to affirm, not to assert; the ability not to get bated. Such is the netherland — the *neitherland* — of Djurić's poems.

Think of these works not as poetry in translation but as poetry in transition, poetry as transformation. Dubravka Djurić's foreignness is near.

Djurić sounds the world as echolocation and expression—oscillating between the Scylla and Charybdis of a turbulent echopoetics.

The Politics of Hope (After the War) is sound writing for an unsound world.

—Charles Bernstein
Election Day 2022
Brooklyn

Note on Translations and Notes

All poems were translated by Biljana D. Obradović except where indicated. Many of the poems were rewritten in English by the poet with the translator (or vice versa). For all other translators or co-translators look at the bottom of each poem:

tr. DD (Dubravka Djurić)
tr. BDO (Biljana D. Obradović)
tr. CB (Charles Bernstein)
tr. JS (James Sherry)

All notes in the book are by Biljana D. Obradović, unless otherwise stated.

Part 1: *Clouds and Shores/Clouds and Shapes, 1982-1983* (1989)[6]

---

[6] When poems are in quotes, it means they did not have titles originally, but we are using their first lines as titles. Also these translations slightly vary from the original translations, but were edited by the translator and author. (DD/BDO)

"After midnight"

After midnight
Different creatures
Gather
At Walpurgis night[7]

tr. DD

"Changes"

Changes
Gray   white   blue
                          sky
Wind currents spread the colors

tr. DD/BDO

"Exhausted"

Exhausted
High above
Towards Artaxerxes, the king[8]

tr. DD/BDO

---

[7] The poem was written by chance operation. The source was the translation of Johann Wolfgang von Goethe's *Faustus*. Walpurgis Night, in German folklore, is the night when witches meet and refers to a chapter of *Faustus*. (DD)

[8] The poem was written by chance operation and the source was the *Bible*. (DD)

"Eyes have touched the sky"

Eyes have touched the sky
Praying for rain
Sadness has overcome the heart

tr. DD/BDO

Prayer for Today

Transform sadness into joy
Let there be no joy
Let there be no sadness

tr. DD/BDO

"Strangely overcast"

Strangely overcast
Is the sky above
Delicate and sensitive
To the touch of our stares

tr. DD/BDO

"Moving my hand I trace the shape of a shell"

Moving my hand I trace the shape of a shell
Meeting everywhere—a whirlpool
Emptiness echoes with longing
For fulfilment

tr. DD/BDO

"Out of a dew the dawn is born"

Out of a dew the dawn is born
Out of a dew the evening is born
Through the dew I walk barefoot
Coldness and wetness become
A part of me

tr. DD/BDO

"I see"

I see
If the space is blue
Let it be
What I see is reflected

tr. DD/BDO

Part 2: *Nature of the Moon/Nature of the Woman— Nine Metapoems (1989)*[9]

[9] The structure of the book was derived from the 12th century book by Rinzai school Zen master Kaku-an Shi-en titled *Ten Oxhering Pictures, forwarded* by D.T. Suzuki. The translation by Belgrade prose writer and translator, David Albahari (1948-2023), appeared in 1979 through Albahari's private edition. The title was translated as *Deset slika o čuvanju bika*. See: https://terebess.hu/english/Kuoan1.html. Analogously, I structured my book in three parts: the first titled "Searching," the second part "Rules" (reference to Kaku-an) and the last "She Is the Other," referring to my interest in feminism from an early age. The interest in Zen Buddhism was part of the intellectual climate of the time, but the main impact in my work came from Mirko Radojičić (1948-2004), a conceptual artist from Novi Sad. (DD)

from Part 1 of "Searching"

2

My dear

My dear

From day to day I write to you

From day to day I write to you

From year to year I write to you

From year to year I write

to you

Lilies
hidden in the grass

In a restaurant you buy me lilies

From day to day I write

From day to day I write

The sand on which I walk is burning hot
I can't stand on it

Screams

Screams

Screams

We swim far away from the coast to the sandy islands
on which you stand and you are above sea level

From day to day I write to you

From day to day I write to you

The number of words overwhelms me
The words knock me down
I can't follow the meaning

Screams

            Screams

                              Screams

We swim to the sandy islands
far away from the coast
It's exciting to stand on them
and to observe the sea

          Laughter
          Laughter

        From year to year

                        From year to year

     Words combine in new ways
     Allowing a new experience

       I am surprised by the variety
       the color of violets
              I mail it in a letter
              the color of violets
    Far from the coast

Screams

            Screams

                              Screams

I am writing to you
        I am writing to you

      From day to day

From day to day

Screams

        Screams

               Screams

Far from the coast
        to the sandy island

At night we pass by the *turbah*[10]
with eternally lit candles
        Through
the iron bars people toss coins

        Violets
    dry violets
           after a few years
      fade

      /violets in the grass/

    hidden word

---

[10] *Turbah*—a turbah (Arabic: soil) is a small piece of soil or clay, often a clay tablet, used during *salat* (Islamic daily prayers) to symbolize earth. The use of a turbah is compulsory in the Twelver Shia school of Islam, a unique practice of the sect, and many Hadiths mention the benefits of prostration on the soil or an alternative natural material. Soil from anywhere may be used. In the absence of soil, plants or items made from plants may be substituted. This provision has been extended to include the use of paper. Prostration must be performed on pure earth or what grows on it. (BDO)

The reference is to the mausoleum in the center of the Adriatic coast town, Ulcinj, in Montenegro with the *turbe* of a fake messiah, Shabbatai Zevi. I spent my early childhood in Ulcinj. During Ottoman times, the Jewish sect, Donme (approximately 5000 people), and their leader, Shabbatslai, returned to Islam, but the Ottomans didn't recognize them, and the Jews renounced them. (Thanks to Montenegrin poet and prose writer, Ruth Stefanović, for this clarification.) (DD)

Repetitions bring about rhythm
An easily recognizable structure

        Far from the coast

        /hidden/

       in the grass

          /a sandy island/

I don't express myself
The I is distanced from the written

Screams

       Screams

           Screams

Words don't carry experience/the adventure
They enable the experience/the adventure

   A long long time

       on the street

         having fainted

           I lie down

   A long long time

       on the street

         having fainted

           I lie down

She recognized me by my dress

                  Far from the coast

           I enter the house through the window

Swallows make their nests

      Screams

               Screams

                                Screams

From day to day

          the shapes change

from day to day

           silence

        Often I say
          the word

         SILENCE

Swallows make their nests

          Far from the coast

          Far from the coast

3

The   flow   of   words   is

              broken

                        The coast is unusually calm

           for   this   time   of   year

                      There is no period

                            No comma

    A few capital letters   and   a bunch of lower case letters
         strung together one after the other

         A rock is surrounded by water
         waves hit it

             The rock shaped like a fish

         Steep approach
               sheep's path

The sentence doesn't have to make sense

         I play

          WITH THE SENSE

        OF NONSENSE

      Rain falls on the sea
      surface
      Rain falls on the sea
      Surface

        Every drop hits the sea

Surface

Music

pure music
of phenomena

DRIP   DRIP   DRIP

DROP   DROP   DROP

Language cannot imitate
the sound of a song / of the sea

even when you say

MURMUR

it's not the same
as when

you hear music
pure music of phenomena

It's unusual to be in the city by the sea in winter again
Memories of the time passed
are unclear

A sentence follows the sense
of words

I play

WITH NONSENSE

OF SENSE

Every word of the speech drowns

32

into

LANGUAGE

The sentence follows the flow of the mind

Syllables
the sounds
whose meaning
is in the rhythm
of the sound

which repeats itself

pure music of phenomena

DRIP   DRIP   DRIP

DROP   DROP   DROP

The coast is unusual for this time of the year
—the sentence which doesn't make sense
doesn't fit the natural order

The slope of the hill

is

the slope of the words

a word disappears in

LANGUAGE

DRIP   DRIP   DRIP

DROP   DROP   DROP
The flow of words is broken

In my nature it is not
a violation of rules of syntax and semantics

Is that fear
in front of

NONSENSE

OF SENSE

?

It's unusual to be back
in this city
in winter
Memories are unclear

Break the meaning of words
Break the meaning of sentences

Each whole is
a view of reality
The rock is covered by the sea
The word is covered by sense

an unusual coast

The flow is broken

It drips

DRIP   DRIP   DRIP

Break the structure

DROP   DROP   DROP

sentences and words

on the surface of the sea
/the surface of sense

it's unusual

to see reality's plans

Play

DRIP   DRIP   DRIP

                    DROP   DROP   DROP

My language experiences
            THE MURMUR
                    OF THE SEA
differently from other languages

The connection between
        the consonants and the vowels
                is unusual
                        in
                    any word

The memory of the beginning
                    is strange

                    Breaking the meaning of
                    WORDS

This city is strange
            But I still have not discovered
            the nature of the connection
            between me and the words
            names and names

WHILE

THE FLOW

IS BROKEN

TERMINATED

DRIP   DRIP   DRIP

DROP   DROP   DROP

4

The sun's ray

On the table cauliflower

I love to ride a bicycle

The completed sentence enters the text

The sun's ray doesn't illuminate
the poem's understanding

I delay lunch for later

She walks down the street

/rain/
She walks over puddles

/sun/

Cauliflower is ready to be eaten
/on the table lunch for the one who is not present/
/absent/

The monster from the tale
I could not tell

paper page / / a sheet of paper

A sentence is a whole

SHE IS ME

I walk in the rain

the cauliflower gets rained on
/sun/

She is the Moon
She is the Earth

Her nature is wet

These sentences don't make sense

Imagine a word
Imagine a sentence

Look at a word
Look at a sentence

Letters appear on things
Letters are the opposite picture of the world

I walk in the rain
Walks in the rain

SHE IS ME

What is the nature of the MOON like?

of an image
What is the nature of the ~~reflection~~

Of the MOON   in   the   lake   ?

What is the nature   of   WORDS   ?

Every word could be
        placed in the poem
Every word could be
        placed in the poem

                    an
                  an I an
                    an

              Break the rules

        BRE   AK!

WILLLL   BREEE   AKKKKK!

        BBBB
              RRRRRRRRR
                    KKKKKKKKKKKKK

I wash under the shower head

              Fish are in the sea
    at certain times during the day they nibble
              by the rocks

              Fish–symbol of Christianity
                –symbol of faith

              I BELIEVE   IN THE WORD

        SHE   IS   THE I   AM   SHE

            SHE IS   AM SHE

This is not A GAME
PLAYING

THIS IS AN IMAGE OF THE MOON MADE OF
WORDS

M O O N
W O O N   in
                    SEA

                    the word   MOON
Rain falls
        I walk in the rain
                    /Moon/
            /and the Sun/
We eat in town
            We eat quickly

Breaking rules
in order to lose the sense

a monster from the tale
I can't tell
The Moon

In the sea
fish

in the sea

I hide like a crab

The poem is an open structure
Writing means filling
paper with marks
of nonsense

I break rules
The image of the world break

MOON

Moon in water,

A MOON FROM WORDS

She is I
Word
Water and fish are merged

The completed sentence enters a text
This is the text of the poem

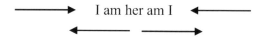 I am her am I

/the arrows show in which direction to read/

from Part 2 of "Rules"

1

Everything is fine
all knowledge just one thread
thread among threads

Sour tendrils of a grapevine

Now is the moment
for a firm decision

Soft dough is stretched

The search cannot be postponed
The search cannot be continued

After some time nothing is the way it is
But it is a trace in the shape of a cloud
It disperses from the heat

The trace disappears

Memory is an ECHO

Aporia of
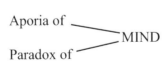MIND
Paradox of

I'm thinking of language
I'm   dreaming of language

Not inspiration   –   TO BREATHE IN
/A BREATH/   breathe IN   –   breathe OUT   /A BREATH/

A ghost appears at night

There are no real events
                    reality (really?)

Warm bread at 4am
in the morning in front of the bakery

                    Avoiding sudden falls
            (the loss of breath)
            (the loss/weakening of inspiration)

                              It's good to follow the good ghost

                Recovery
            Following a trace

                    Taming down language[11]
            The taming of the bull/language is the self
collective selves

        All knowledge is only a thread
            Motives disappear
                    Don't appear
                        Don't intertwine
                                    Don't return
            In the rhythm of a repeated sound
/when time passes I have to write/
                    /writing develops out of writing/

            Avoid of the set guidelines
            Avoid the given inspiration
        It's unnecessary for a poem to appear.

---

[11] Taming—"Taming down the language," refers to Taming the Buddhism Kakuan, "Ten Images of Taking Care of a Bull."

2

A poem is not sung
It's a mental exercise
The logic of searching

The logic of place

The dynamic of being static
The static of the dynamics of the mind

The second approach is marked by the trace

I don't express the feeling
I don't express the experience

Not the sadness
Not the pain
Not the happiness

Without passion
steady
exploration of

LANGUAGE

MIND

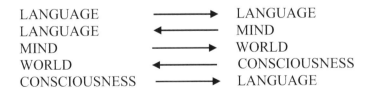

LANGUAGE ⟶ LANGUAGE
LANGUAGE ⟵ MIND
MIND ⟶ WORLD
WORLD ⟵ CONSCIOUSNESS
CONSCIOUSNESS ⟶ LANGUAGE

I discard

the straightforward

interpretation

There is no straightforward motion

Language is a liquid surface
The axis of the language breaks

The vision

from ALL POINTS INTO ALL DIRECTIONS

3

In itself [12]

a bare surface

by itself it (is) only (with) it (self)
it is/is
into the un/known <known>
on the path/s <at>

echo it is what it is

---

[12] The early conceptual poetry and conceptual texts by Vladimir Kopicl especially his book of poetry/texts *Aer* (Matica srpska, 1978) were crucial in writing *Priroda meseca/Priroda žene* [*Nature of the Moon/ Nature of the Woman*]. (DD)

for the sound of

language is/age is it is

only a small part of me

alienated

outside of
above
language
(from)
language

is by itself/herself/himself/me/myself

3

The logic of operations
does <not> include the interference of the self
as the one which is self-expressive

The logic of operations
does <not> include the interference of the self
as the one which is self-expressive

In the extremes
In the rift
and the hiatuses

No disruption is absolute

Language follows the logic of language/mind
But the world is divided into many languages,
many selves, and each is a kind of a general
self of language in which it participates and which
enables it

Reduce language to the pure relationship
of language and language
of language and mind

The processes of the mind are logical processes
which reduce the language of the mind to it/itself
/meta—language of the mind/

To feel language by the language itself
/meta—language of the mind/

She Is the Other (Part One)

ONLY
ONE TYPE OF
UNDERSTANDING ONLY
ONE TYPE OF VISION
I ≠ EYE = I OF LANGUAGE

ONLY BY BREAKING OUT
OF THE FRAMEWORK OF WHAT HAS BEEN ACHIEVED

ONLY BY BREAKING OUT OF THE NORMS

I OF LANGUAGE

= I OF LANGUAGE

I ≠ EYE

I ≠ EYE = I OF LANGUAGE

I ≠ I

ARCHETYPAL SYMBOL OF YIN YANG
UNITES OPPOSITES

WHAT IS THE NATURE OF THE MOON
WHAT IS THE NATURE OF WOMEN
WHAT IS THE NATURE OF THE QUESTION

She Is the Other (Part Two)

THE PURPOSE OF LANGUAGE IS TO POINT
OUT TO ITSELF
THE PURPOSE OF LANGUAGE IS TO POINT OUT
/TO POINT/

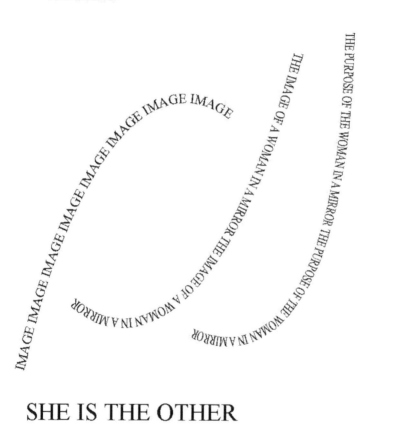

SHE IS THE OTHER

With Oneself

WITH HERSELF
ALONE
(I) AM AN IMAGE

/AN IMAGE OF MYSELF
IN A MIRROR/

ON THE EDGE OF THE CIRCLE ON THE EDGE ON THE EDGE OF THE CIRCLE ON THE EDGE ON THE EDGE OF THE CIRCLE ON THE EDGE

SHE IS

HERSELF   A PURPOSE

ONTO

Part 3: *Stretching the Frames/Slash of/Context, 1988-1990* (2020)[13]

---

[13] from Dubravka Djurić's *Razmicanje okvira/ Kosa crta/ Konteksta, 1988-1990* (OrionArt, 2020), published in 2020, but written much earlier (1988-1991).

The title refers to the texture of the book that worked with different contexts of radical art and poetry, including Yugoslavian conceptual art's textuality, Russian Cubo-Futurism, Russian Formalism, reading and investigating James Joyce and Language poetry. The title of the first part "Stasis/Shifts" points to the word *stasis* taken from Charles Bernstein's text "Writing and Method" and Barrett Watten's text "Method and *L=A=N=G=U=A=G=E*," both published in Ron Silliman (ed.), *In the American Tree: Language, Realism, Poetry* (University of Maine at Orono, 1986). Both texts were translated by me and published in Belgrade's journal *Delo* no. 8 in 1989, dedicated to American Poetics. Shifts refers to Aleksei Kruchyonykh *здвиг* referring to syntactic and semantic shifts. The work with line in Ron Silliman's *new sentence* was also important. (DD)

Eye Around Everything[14]

                         oblivion moves on
RHYME RHYTHM ---------------the edge of a word consciousness is blurred

                         crystal cleans on the bottom
HAND RHYTHM -----------------earth fire vomits

                         arm moves towards the bottom
HORN RHYTHM ----------------the edge of consciousness murky water

                         fish arm consciousness mud
SYLLABLE RHYTHM ---------to the bottom to the bottom

         There darkness darkens
                til darkness ---------------water
                        leads with water
                        to the bottom

           springing up sizzling very searing and seawater
                  are home

               to the bottom to the bottom
                breathing that cheers

no end
flows flows ----------------------
word towards
water leads

---

[14] From: Stazis/ Pomeranja.
This poem was written having in mind the books by Sanja Marčetić, a poet from Zagreb, who wrote under the influence of Russian Cubo-Futurism. At the beginning of the Yugoslavian civil war, Marčetić moved to Sweden and never came back. Her work is still important for me. (DD)

into twilight
        happens
darkness

----

                                    towards water lead
                                    where fire and water
                                    are home to the wind

        lion's roaring

w
a   d
t   r   f
e   i   r   w
r   p   o   a   o
    s   m   l   f
            l
            s   c
                a
                v
                e
                s

        Mighty old mighty Silen[15]
            word breaks
                    in the mouth
                spit   flows
                    the nest of fire
                                quiet shelter
                    exactly that he said

MY PATH IS THE PATH OF WORDS

---

[15] Silen—mythical figure, a god of woodland.

56

clear thought clearly said
it's ringing   it rings

        in the cave of words

hidden

       /the water drips on the wall drips/
      humidity wets the stare
              with the touch
MY PATH IS THE PATH OF WORDS
      the paths di-
          verge

Image distorted

               an image in the water
------------------   an image in the mirror
               an image of an image
               a reflection
                    shadow

               the trace has not been lost

I have seen the cave
the entrance covered with branches

        the thunder's sanctuary
        the sanctuary of words
        of fire and water
        exit

     MY PATH IS THE PATH OF WORDS

towards the bottom

coral

     light

        pearl

it squeaks   and   screeches

                pours

to the bottom

        to the bottom

The Border

Nothing remains halfway which has crossed a certain path tends to go towards the end in the unspoken even though the words are always there to say what cannot be said in the telling. Because the road once traveled is traveled again with a different type of memorable experience or without it traces are imprinted in the body of words the body of bodies / of the sky and of the earth because one is the Moon's body the other the Sun's body as is the human body and that of animals / they move under different laws guided by a forethought of consciousness or without it because the word is the cause of all movement.

And beginning again from the starting point means movement in the same or a different direction but it is never identical to itself and when it is identical it is different in itself for itself and according to that beyond itself that it gets its meaning which even when it is is not the cause on its own.

Disordering

1.

   Lackadaisical   paradox   drowns   itself
imagines   eats   stares
same's same   always and now
                          later is what's left on the table
mother and father   later's the same
      knows it's happening haphazardly
with plain want hurtling at
                  so am shutting shutters
to shower on fire   later freezes itself.

2.

   Not a wish—fear of a flower
wilted faded mole moldering
      from a one to one   multitude as such
is here from seed (things) thing in mind
magnitude
            wish's wish dries, breaks
                  if it is only lonely in doubt
same's in empty room
                        silence.

3.

   Simply spit out name's names
I give myself to names not apparently in
words names' letters gave for names
my names in you spit out.

4.

   Later every day follows the day inside
Upside down on floors between doors upsidedown
once happened but not again when it's
upsidedown later everyday is.

5.

   Don't ask questions in brackets among

rows of trees /among rows of trees/ in tedious rhythm
monotonous stringing down the hill but only
to see rows like the reflection of wish and want like
circling in circles a sentence behind and in front is and
it is because continuity
word on word leans in meaning and symbolically
the same process is always only the stress
removed from that side behind or in front
above or below the same is.

Tr. CB/BDO [16]

---

[16] In this version I added a line that was missing (third from the bottom) and returned the
original spacing and capitalization of lines. (BDO)

Disordering (2)[17]

joyful   hotspots   focal leg temple
i eat   stand   stay   quiet   from   the same   towards
   an arm   swing the same   with a leg   eats
by the   square   squirrel in time   doesn't   eat   hour
 under   the flat   in the floor   time is   that now/how an hour
an inscription description   onto the street   a bicycle   a wheel   of the sun
i doubt for   the continuation without and with   and   the twilight
wind
  blind blindness an image   colors and   words   bound together
still and yet   and if and because and as soon as   and behind
be hind   the swing i waved   moved away   the glass
  a miracle   a sandal   a roof a river   eats   sky   need for   needy
not the usual no i and eye don't have   any not a bit   an hour   in
time under   the square on the square behind belate   it moves
scowls
       a sister   and a room after itself with   me it is
is it leaves   a lot   where   the morning is   at the foothill
  the eye is   alone and it is   and is heavy with earth's gravity
heavier than the heaviest   sister is a cut   heavier   gravity
     the day   doesn't   begin   the same branches window   shadow
 therefore it is   so   visible   a tear   happiness eats table
eats   at a table   raise   a glass   is   on the clock   is
       from   one   row
             into   another
the arm   is on   water between   the air   if it is   like   that it is
i envy i see   smoke   that's why   it's like that   sister an hour is
 it is stayed behind   streetlamp   is what it   is
       is an arm
         on silk
            on the sand
     is a leg is a head   eats

---

[17] This poem was created after translating fragments for a publication in 1989 Belgrade's literary journal, *Delo*, from the book by Hannah Weiner, *Spoke* (Sun & Moon Press, 1984), published in Silliman's *In the American Tree*. (DD)

left   and   right
              in-between
                      rows
                              can be seen
to manage   more   difficult   doesn't   handle
     from the same direction
                                        doesn't stop
     that's   why   the city   is the same as   and   the clock   an hour   in time
when   it doesn't   arrive   beside   the square   because   the earth's gravity
doesn't stop moves   besides the language   the tongue   on the brink   the
verge   that   merges
       the name   is   that   which   says   itself   arm follows   one
     if it is like   that the sense   is
                                              on
the water discouraged   bitten   eats   hour   in
       water   worried   on   time   hour   in   time
     is time   in   an hour   is
           at   the bus   stop   at   noon
                  time   has stopped   at noon
       accidentally
i am searching   for the sequel   heat   warmth   melts
       said he   a trace   i   was
is   eating   her
         on   her   own   sister   is   not   a word   on a hand
   wrist   finger   tightened
             is   thinking   itself
       is   searching   itself

Stasis[18]

She paused. On the threshold. Among other things. She paused. Tortured. Between words. Yes. Left out. Yes. In between. In between petals. Words. She paused. Is. Is. Stopped. Remained. In between flower buds. New word. New. I repeat the same. The same. Statement. Everything is the same. Is the same. Everything. Left out. Paused. Dangling in between. If it is. Is in between. I recognize the statement. I write. Writing is. Traveling. Through words. Sentences. Paused in between. Words. Sentence. Paused. Surprised. The same repeats itself. Itself again. Repeats itself. Again is the same. The same. Standstill. From. Towards. Again the same. Is. A flower is a word is a rose has paused is in a deadlock between the word flow. Remained. I am. Wrote. Went out. Went. Faced with. Faced. A flower bud is a word. A word is a tale is a tale. I found myself amid. A forest of words. A physical touch with. Words. Emptied meaning. Removed. Meaning. Removed. She stopped. Left. Is a thought. Fell out of. Behind herself. Be. Out of herself. Out of. Behind. Disturbed. In the middle of. Disturbed. In the middle of. Disturbed. Stopped. Stopped in front of. In front of. In front of me. She stared. Looked at. At herself. In the middle of herself. Word. The surface. Superficial. No. Remains unchanged. How is it the same? The same. Again. Is. Because of. If it is. She left. Stopped. In the middle of. Confused. Condensed. Neglectful. Consciously. Swayed in darkness. Dark solitude. Silky. In the middle of the night. A forest of words. In the indirectly unspoken. Newly uttered. Stasis. Water-word-level. Water-level. Writing is. Searching. Behind the words. In front of words. Word-descending. Low-descendings. I am hiding word creation in the spoken-on-the-written. Rose is a froze is a word. Periodlettered. Slanted. Plotted. At the table stopped at the table stopped squeezing the table the chair. Lost herself. Frog. Dog. Prologue. Word. Left out. Installed. Behind. Equal-limbed word. Word-limbed. Stopped. Elephoned. Removed. Pursued. Wanted. Turned around. Moved around. Oh. Alone. Around. Alone. I am. I by myself. Bent. A fairy. Flat. Inverted. Began moving. Being moved. Stopped. At the table. Statement. Is. Repeated. Again. Over. Repeated. Is. Is in a row. Not-that-it-is-in the-row. Til the end. Til.

---

[18] This and the next poem were written at the time when I was translating parts of Lynn Hejinian's *My Life*. (DD)

Shifts

That remained to be done. Moving from the dead end. Phrases that are repeated and mean without meaning. Arm on the table. Writing from day to day. I'm restraining a wish. Self-reflection. A priori set requirements. Dreams. If dreams are messages, to understand them, I need to decipher them. Every sign, material or not, is a letter, needed to be deciphered. Deciphering implies many different interpretations. I looked over the accomplished with the knowledge that I of the writer is multifaceted and that it acts. I placed a period. Turned over to a new page. Began a New Life.[19] Symbols only help to understand it. As an empty phrase an empty symbol. Emptiness is wear and tear, a shell, an empty form. Matter needs form in order to shape itself. Creation implies already existing elements which can be restructured. Combining elements in different varieties gives different elements the same, similar or opposite types. I glanced over the already completed—in order for the written/spoken sentence to function like a leitmotif and therefore given the rhythm to the already written text. I turned a page over in order to start a New Life over. New elements reshape the old. What's left to do is to vary the limited number of elements. That's why I placed a period. So that the new sentence could begin again. So that a New Life of words would begin in the portion of the texture of the text. The meaning is the same. When it exists.

---

[19] "New Life" is a reference to Dante, through T.S. Eliot and Ezra Pound. (DD)

You Are My Heart[20]

A white platform falls. I sit and eat. An hour. A solar clock in the sea. Five, six. Twilight. Three times three. Everything comes down to that. Leaves in a lens. The edge of sorrow in a shadow. If the multiplied gets what is wanted. Wish for. Breathing. Yellow fluff. Water in water. A look and then a swing. Three times into the same is the same. Five and one. Seven mirrors in an inverted position. Seven looks at a mirror. One and three. After seven finally in itself. That's why six in breathing gives three times tie in turn. Think of six in one and there a hundred in itself. A white platform falls into the heart of darkness. Seven and seven into one. From darkness in three is five in the lake. On the hill a garden and vineyard. On the hill a hill in seven entwined into a word. Three times folded in itself it reflects the world. In the darkness the heart in three ends the dream is an emptiness five times transformed.

---

[20] From: Part two, *Knjiga brojeva/ Book of Numbers.*
For this part of the book, reading Ludwig Wittgenstein's *Tractatus* was important. Wittgenstein's work was important for Yugoslavian analytical conceptual art as well as for Language poets. (DD)

My Little Heart

Blue stretches out into the fog. Wind inscribed into the color scatters feathers. In the cliff a spinning top can be spotted. An abstract number in the echo of the voice. Two divers and one. Diving in the sea he comes up fogged up with the mixture of salt, water and minerals. Leaves of seaweed and a sea spider. Four-leaf in four blue ones. Nuance in one circles around a number from the fog evaporated in the fog of rain. One is a six after four will appear the nine. Three-leafed in three blooms green water in blue disappears white gravel. Fog is inside gray gravel of abstract number of the transparent. An imaginary number added to itself into a sickle draws a moon. Painted in four with the shadow of the heart.

Passages

i don't convey meaning on the surface stirring the influence of water wind and sun in the constellation of sea stars spider's web path through the forest leads to the top of the hill from where a vista extends the beginning and the end in the number and in between confusion a rocky demolished edifice an olive tree in the rock pile not the past or the future remains only a trace of powder in the number nine through growth the existent sand slides through the hands of matter rots words fall apart so that not even a trace remains the lost falls into the sand there are words which tell me that which they can articulate slanted i climb on the steep side a thought of the possibility tells me what could be in a closed room darkness a device is a word which says don't speak in silence because meaning melts like ice in the sun if i stated that in order to confirm the same occurs with words because the star is the same in the word transformed into veins the roots hold the tree trunk upright in itself closed world doesn't open easily but the stone is rough cold and gray or covered in moss wet and green in water and mossy slimy and slippery think of the word and body in the zero gravity space water doesn't grind but instead floats decomposition is postponed but matter changes she has gone mad from the pain when the world disappears in the word how do i understand the speech in silence the smoldering glare of colors change with time at the moment i am looking at the grass as the blades of grass bend in the wind in the poem silence doesn't speak in a language that makes sense but instead breaks into shards they bring luck you smile and even though you're sad the word doesn't say do this now or let it go at noon it's time to take a rest and tomorrow everything is not the same because there are no changes from day to day time affects the changing of shape and meaning i see myself but that's not me because in the word i have died[21] but the word only says i have died in you in order that i could be i on paper and the sun in the poem and its embodiment in the sacred word and the sacred sign of the cultures die and with them words and meanings but we read traces wrong only the threshold remains and the sand slides down the hands and a dove watches the spectacle and sadness is sadness in the word because the beginning and the end touch one another at the same point and the point is the horizon in the word the intersection from both ends of the star field in the

---

[21] Refers to Michael Palmer's *Sun*. (DD)

68

sky and in the night field[22] every source of light is a double for stars but the sea stars in the word are the same as everything else because one adds to the other in order to understand the logic of stringing the word collapses into debris which brings happiness and happiness is a fragile material that rots in time there is no trace left except for dust and the ruin is the remnant of a world that i know nothing about because it acts upon me unconsciously mechanically i act in the space because nothing could be seen in space nor in time nothing remains not even a trace of water stands in the recess but form doesn't shape the content nor does content shape form but all that is happening is in the relativity of meaning from this and the other side the same is also happening that ties are looser thin spiderwebs in the sun and the dew wets the grass while the echo echoes through the landscape and silence echoes forcefully in the ear if you are not a good receiver sand disperses while the humidity gnaws at the tree and the rock is lined you don't notice change it just disappears and you don't know what has happened and why it's the way it is when all encompasses everything the sounds of birds animals people noise of motored boats a sign that carries a message dies the message is unclear the sign is activated in various vectors of meanings' flow run forking rivers or sea currents mixing hot and cold water from both sides numbers multiply the earth crumbles the plant in the crack of a stone springs and its roots spread and the little ground for a sign in a letter blooms a flower and the meaning changes because the surface is rough and hard textured and not transparent not the world before the words but the world in words

---

[22] This refers to conceptual OHO's project by Milenko Matanović, "The constellation of candles in the field corresponds to the constellation of the stars in the sky." April 30, 1970. (DD)

"death looked at itself into the eyes…"

death looked at itself into the eyes p comes out of q the coast differs from all wasting of time in death the landscape of speech and q gets lost into p the same remains unchanged in its original meaning a stream springs and fresh water with its healing effects calms down the need for counting the silver thread of a spider web in the sun and the darkness eats the sun creatures spider comes out of a hole and the scorpion is still on the wall the snake tucks into an opening of a stone rock by rock fall into the empty space silence and thought slither on the bow and the arrow shot pierces the air the still body doesn't exist the soul has freed itself in the dream from an irreversible condition a cry tears off in the echo transmuted crying the log falls and rolls on the ground ants carry the dead body of a grasshopper motion inscribes signs in arm movements an empty paper is filled a word follows a word and already meaning is constituted in death words speak in the world where the trace hides a trace new layers cover old in layers of earth arranged on the earth meaning leans on meaning the world empties itself when there are no words and fills up when they are present in one move the world gets ruined through words three meanings don't include all possibilities reduced to one stone is dust and the ground under the arm a trace on paper and in death's space ashes are scattered all over the earth meaning dies til its uncertain death

"Logic that describes…"

Logic that describes movement over the sections of the lawn and the stone pile signifies zero degree of your existence. Noise doesn't add to the description of all possibilities during a single unique action: synchronous moving of the arms and legs during the advance through space lasts eternally. Because it returns to the starting point certain in the uncertainty of events in language, the moment is a dot in space, time flows uninterrupted through it.

Space is:
Peek with your head through the window
The loss of balance
The landslide is collapsing
Helplessness
In Berlin you cannot be alone
Loneliness is the same everywhere
As is incapacity
Change the water in a vase
Water flower pots
The grass is burnt from the heat, flowers dried up
At the same time no one speaks
Work will help you to get over it
Sadness is humidity swallows hearts

I am confused by the fact of death
Like birth--the start and the finish
Begin with an equal sign in between.
The symbol of nothing.

"Churches are domes…"

Churches are domes of numbers. A sum of signs in the stone of words.
The vast area of transformation. The sum of life and an image on
the doors. The color fades in the sun. Grey of eight dreams in the stone.
While language of motion speaks in a dance of the elements. The fire is
a word in the flame of paper. The moon with the tide paints movement. Not
final til fulfillment. Filled circle reflected by the moon. In
zero the totals are added. Subtract everything added. Five and three in
nine with two multiplied by zero in the tripled sky dome.

"A fingerprint is imprinted..."

A fingerprint is imprinted in the crack

The crack covers space

The space is coated with pigment

The direction points to absence

Abstract relations in a given situation

Event hinted by uncertainty

Dislocated and unarticulated

The nature of that is in that

That is divided by a fraction

Multiplication is subtracted by division

Upright and vertical on the back

White marble with black letters

Every fact enters indirectly

The sum of the facts is the summary of words

During which I don't think about the logical flow of events

During which I don't think about the unique meaning of an individual
statement

Or the sum of individual statements

Part 4: from *Traps* (KOV, 1995)

"Messenger of embers..."[23]

Messenger of embers, poets of veil
metric devices, lazy sights
Logic of growth and close
Tolling hill-spires topple
Sunrise at sea, twilight of nightmares
Hatred flares, lightning the maze of cages
Smooth bond in a split knot

Cut the prism, strip the firefly, sacred vengeance revenged
Madly murmurs the sea
conversation pretty, seductive
one-way
Lines, knives, doors, merry-go-rounds
Wreaths of death, ring around the rosy
Heights hang, jokes thrown down in poison intrigues
Graves—graveyards of lives
Castle—germs of love
Smashed fragile towers
stamen-haven
flaming-amen
crushed

Little intrigues knit the chain
opponent-slogans fall alive into graves
Sluggish witches, merry snowdrops

Round dances[24] make the world go round

Crucify fructify, vivider divots
of homes, of rivers and angry roofs

Feeds, weeds, tweeds
Rubber, lubber, bullets, nuggets, druggist

---

[23] Previously published in *ProFemina* as "From *Traps*," Special Issue 1997, pp. 133-4.

[24] Round dances: *kolo,* a Serbian folk dance, shared by many Balkan nations.

Stares, fights of clear glare
Vid[25] and Vida can see again
Sheep harnessed
Yoke of sultriness
Veils of malice
and fines

Enemies ingenious fathers, dresses, glasses
Debtors of limbs mangle laps and kneecaps
tearing their dewy hairs
Clowns rise and glow
and liberty from Hades laughs
HA HA HA HA HA
Fights between words narrate
"Words in freedom" submit to new meters
killers
secretly burn'n'turn skeleton's lunacy
fragile madness in crops broke

for the ode
for the line
fragile pine
of "new epics"

Carefully wrapped up in white drifts
we climb the glade
burning snows and white hills
they thaw and flood
sinned infant of a quill

Receive penitence, be penitent
Purify yourself in the white flame of the snowstorm
Burn the face, picture of the self

---

[25] *Vid*, a male name, also means "sight" in Serbian and other languages in the Yugoslavian and post-Yugoslavian speaking areas; I include this because Vida was a common Serbian female name, whereas Vid was a Slovenian male name. The whole collection is antiwar. (DD)

"White, white, everything is white"[26]

fire of pain exiles thought
Burn burnt place of thoughts
flood the wishes, burning
into burnt transmutes body and ground

Three times I turn around
Three times I pray

Abysses gape
put down their hats

Spaces swallow failures, frozen fingers

Gold, golden coins of dawn
sounds, waker of gongs
splits of throne
Threefold
Twofold
of bipolar, three-polar language
notations of soundlessness flow in ether

We rise on our tip-toes to see the prospect
language hermaphrodite
drunken, secret, severe

Sum of three words
Power of this code

Brims, boundaries, norms, dogmas
shells, scale, skin

"I am a cupola of your body

---

[26] This refers to the work of Croatian poet, Sanja Marčetić, who left Yugoslavia at the beginning of the Yugoslavian civil war. During the 1980s, her work, relying on Russian Cubo-Futurist poetry, was important for me. See earlier footnote 14. (DD)

I am all white"
I am all daring
since I reduce
all knowledge to taboo
all forbidden to flow
which flows above the dawn
above the sea and abyss
above glare of the invisible
darkened chorus out of abyss
of starry hell of language-gathering

And it is the body of stars, woods, vales
body of death in a dream of a poem
shallow borders, dough of body
by modest shape it is intended
toward the infinity of unseen
toward horrible sound of glosses
and clear dawns

New suns
New dawns
New stars
Towers of bodies
Cone of pens
Of golden coins and flowers
Tides of pain
Low, careful
Look

The bells are comatose
Voices do not voice
Stuffy silence
Reasonable mist-lava

Some twinkle anchored in the harbor of collusion

breaches, seizure, thunders
lightning, sabers, blades

keep the trembling
hush the necklace
fasten the leech
bloody poem of plea

Death, death, death
sings a song

Swept words, swept rhymes, swept rhythms

I destroy words, I destroy rhymes, I destroy rhythms
gigantic, wild, stray

I kiss the all-observing eye
I collect prisms slipped
I beat meters-vagabonds
pale, bloodless
I am your servant, Oh, Word
Let the blood bleed
and take off the sickness of fury

Clear little river floods into sentences
brook—talk
talk—took

Steeples of hell, fields of darkness
Steeples-skeletons of death
Lava lichen, ludicrous
Shapes-shades are mounted on the ground
The cursed cordons cut out
ghosts march,
deduced to a destiny,
fate and darkness
and day of judgement
welcomes them with laughter
deadly deaths
burned up, heartless, soul keepers'
you are the debtors of fate
messengers of judgements

Give amnesty!
Bestow indulgences
to the simple death!

1992

Tr. DD/JS [27]

---

[27] Biljana D. Obradović corrected the British spellings into American. James Sherry translated the poem into American English, but a British editor changed it into British English for the *ProFemina* journal publication. (DD)

Part 5: from *Cosmopolitan Alphabet* (1995)[28]

---

[28] This is not translated but composed from found material from various books published in English.

The End of Language

1. THE END OF REFERENCE

It was in the cooling hour
Red sun sinks down behind
Upon the other, and the rosy sky
I cannot see what flowers
I cannot see
the very world
Up the hillside
Was it a vision or a waking dream?
This is not the place to pursue this thought any further
But men were neither sufficiently mature nor educated for this
magnificent kingdom. With emotions of horror and grief.
After the pause of a moment … the gleams, thrown between the arches
… which was pictured at the grave … the night was stormy … took her
candle … it was black and yellow … it was very odd … the manuscript,
what could it contain? First, the City. The island of the City. The City,
first fell upon the eye with its stern to the east and its prow to the west.

only in this case	beautiful square
over the southern side	its roof
then to the left	tall miters
to the right	intervals and bridges

When we speak of nature in this manner, we have a distinct but most
poetical sense in mind. Not the sun or the summer alone, but every
hour and season yield its tribute of delight. In good health, in snow
puddles, at twilight, under a clouded sky, in the woods within these
plantations of God, standing on the bare ground, when the lake was too
rough, murmur of the waves, the flux of the water.

The roots inside
The shadow of death
Before it, deathbed

Over and back
Over and back
I said

clouds and sand and winds and waves and skies
give me things
sliding screens
I'd like to say and do
Split mind
I wanted to tell
It was dark
down and down
It was dark
over and over
I felt that I began then to feel
Do you see what I mean?
while I was writing
I have finished that
Now what other things are there beside
Beside that there they work
One does do without it
I absolutely do not like it
I feel no regret
Let us begin with these
When I first began beside that period and I don't care now
Let us begin with
The miracles that magic will perform
From martial justice on thy wretched soul
Whose eyes shot fire from their ivory bowers
and sooner let the fiery element dissolve
ALL MOVE FROM EAST TO WEST
ALL MOVE FROM EAST TO WEST
angle slide your hand
the master of the book of lights
the master of the book of numbers
face to face
I heard the stony cry
I came here
I was the moon
Unlike trees or their roots it has neither beginning nor end
It is not made of units but of dimensions or rather of shifting
directions

I am responsible for Utopia in my very desire
Verb, winter, word
Words were flying in all directions. All these on my forehead words are
seen

              seen across the line
            didn't write about it   That means nothing
other
than reorganizing and replicating the existing structures
           I was energy without end
            I was over the line
          I smell the stench of wounds
    Your you is also You, though You might be Them to you
Language is not the instrument of expression, but the substance. All
meaning is a construct, built from the determinate code of language.

The End of Eastern European Poetry[29]

1.

            everything is in good shape
      you sleep
          knowing nothing
              no more idea into valley

don't
      above my head
         a time of loss
            love was born

      in the past

           the flood of light
               and ancient chant

when people meet
         in my own vanishing
            whispers
      within my flesh
         you salute me
            in shadows
                      white ithaca
        like silver over the entrances
      every grief

        any harm
         i still feel your touch

high up   the sky   i invented

---

[29] Source material for this poem was the anthology *Shifting Borders: East European Poetry of the Eighties*, edited by Walter Cummins (Fairleigh Dickinson University Press, 1993). (DD)

the sun, the wind, the moon, the river
their roots deep in the earth
                    your father, hanged
              empty and naked   don't scream
        will speak
the wounds are real

        many nationalities but no nations
in its mood and form
                          nationalism
        share the trauma and nostalgia of the past deeply in love with
her land
                      a need to fill in the lacunae
              ocean of time   like a wolf
                                      bitter   endless

          edged in a circle

                                you only used me

              and the window

                                    sometimes they die

            nothing remains of the first sentence
                          i don't remember

knowing nothing of this   a blue eye
              new dress   you slept

        sick inside

                    new dress   sick inside
                          you slept

a blue eye

nothing remains
        and the window
               like an ocean

sometimes they die
        no nations
            every grief

sick inside

   and the window

      new dress
        bitter

you slept   lacunae
     inside   and the window
       like and ocean

in the soil of the land
     a hyena and madman
        i am only sick

in a stony desert
     after snake
     the dream
       the spirit

a dot in the world
       in the ash of the shadow
     there was a bridge
     there was a temple

i see it and do not see it
      it's all here   through the door
peace, peace, pears, plums
      wild roses
    no one needs your history
      the sound of abyss

the emptiness goes
a dot
      in a stony desert
         it's all here

in the dream
      there was a temple
         peace, peace, pears, plums

there was a bridge
      in the ash of the shadow   i am only sick
         wild roses

through the door

    you slept   it's all here   i see it

in the soil of the land
      sick inside
         nothing remained

after snakes   there was the bridge
         in the sound of the abyss

inside   you slept in the lacunae

      a hyena and madman

it's all here
      in the lacunae

    grass is another metaphor

mirror made of grass
    woman made of glass
         i see myself

i am a circle
      i am a castle

2.

      old is
          empty town   of horrors

the white gleam

      poor town
         death is above the landscape

the blind sacrament
         wounded beats
            of blood and earth
we could no longer wait   here in the past
     silence
         sunset
           in the dark i think

the sense, the sense, the sentence
       and a poem
       of horrors

in the soil of the dream
         there was a bridge
     and a poem and a bridge

peace, peace, like an ocean   in the ash   through the door

no one needs your stony desert
         it's all here   new dress and lacunae
     like the window   i can see   only sick
                     above the landscape

      of blood and earth

        a monument and a prison

without a sound
                    shadow and the face of gold

          we were starving

               my dear
All the buildings around us were burned out
i don't remember the pain
               dry forest burn
                         the velvet of senses the velvet of sentences
               of no return

disappear

          the marble tomb
                    silence and silk
a hunting scene

          in such a dark

                              white ithaca

humans not flowers
                    humans and flowers
          of blood and sunset
                    i don't remember the pain
                    above the landscape

i see myself
                    mirror is another metaphor

towns of horrors
                    a dot and a poem

new dress in ash   burned out

          i don't remember the velvet of no return
a monument and dry forest

only sick like window

of earth no longer
            in its mood and form
like endless edge of the first sentence
            you slept after snakes
knowing nothing of madmen
            we were sick inside
      empty naked   and a prison
                              in the dark

      to silence their voices
                  turn grey   in the grass

that agony of wind

                        the sun never sets there
   through the glass   covered with snow
in a circle   if i say

      i am afraid of dreams
                  of visions   do not ask
in the wind   people were dying   among trees

      the experience of exile is another metaphor

Part 6: from *All Over*, 1996-2004 (2004)

Reflection[30]

The freezing seas of love, don't remain indifferent in passion
between the reflection and the phantasmal grimace of
the jester, the smallest among the toys, is wiping teary eyes
and laughs staring at the disembodied spheres.

Lions, from the constellation, gone wild, spew fire into a deserted
corner of the city, hordes of wild boars, hordes of wild dogs
on the streets.

Out of the foam she emerged: mouth mild skin folds, under the
                                                  microscopically
thin shadows of skyscrapers, she bends so that she can see
the terrified who rush to the place where they are not,
everything but an illusion, it's clear that that is the price I pay

The gravesite in the middle of the city gapes like a crater, devastated alleys,
the avengers are emptying themselves, dwarfs come out of the forest
looking identical to one another, and so into infinity
the sea of hope floods the alleys, Ocean-Father
Moon's trace,
moon's excrement,
mixed with indecipherable signs
melted in undefined matter which sucks everything into itself
a drunk bench with those who've fallen asleep,
parks, fountains disgorge reflections like soft traces of storms
after the rain, after orgies, the deserted city.

Objects are dancing mysterious dances:
chair and table,

---

[30] From the first part of the book titled: *All-Over*, Fusion of Chain Collision (part one) [Fuzija lančanih sudara (prvi deo)] and Insinuations (View into the Future), Belgrade, 1996-7 [Insinuacije (Pogled u budućnost) Beograd, 1996-7]. The whole book deals with the Yugoslavian civil war and is deeply political. (DD)

computer in a trance trembles,
diskettes have paved the podium
From the Ocean-Father the Law springs up
Shaking it off
that dark wish grows out from the foam
The Law
and: the Loan.

Games

dangerous areas   panic of the purified   hidden in the house
behind secret curtains   fogged windows   shadows of
the invisible   inhabit a pirate island of loneliness
        Behind the fence that hides the gardens
        behind gardens that hide secrets, personal secrets
        of dolls which feed on honey in snake litters
with small necklaces
        dangerous areas, areas of anxiety
made up headaches, eye dryness, gap
        between generations, new sensibilities,
"I'm leaving"; "you're leaving"; "they're leaving"
        on a journey, I'm dreaming of a journey, the journey is
                      dreaming of me
this song is so nice, enchanting, seductive
to be there on the spot, to be spotted, as a teary fire of the moon which
spews reflections
like a reflection that radiates horror
Mournful Main[31], aromatic Main
there's no such place to hide
behind the ski equipment behind the fishpond, silver light
reflections, mystically matched with the patterns on lichen
high above this peace, under the shoulder pads
"How did she manage?" "Look, how did she get upset?" "How does she
                      handle loneliness?"
"What she looks like" "How she holds herself"
        The trams have stopped. Trolleybuses have stopped running. People
                      are coming out, and walking.
The pedestrian zone. The magic zone. The twilight zone. The twilight of
                      idols.

Idleness.

---

[31] *Žalostna Majna* by Iztok Geister Plamen is a book, published in 1969 in Ljubljana, of reistic (*reism* is the doctrine that only things exist) poetry. Plamen is a member of the Slovenian conceptual OHO group and a birdwatcher. Majna, in Slovenian, refers to the river, Main. *Acridotheres tristis*. Thanks to Slovenist, Darja Pavlič, for this clarification. (DD)

I'm Growing Out of Well Depths

I'm growing out of well depths
I dive into the embrace of the anteater painted on the burdock plantation
all that is outlined onto the graves of the famous rulers
who bloodied their swords
and ended with chopped heads

I take the world too seriously
then there's no laughter
my very stance makes fun of me
my statement grabs me by the neck:
"too abstract!"
"too gloomy!"

I walk down the street of fear, fear keeps me company
these are the witches' hours, as once in a song with instructions
we were asking which is the most efficient formula

how to make poisonous wine in which all vandals of the world would
     disappear
a poisonous thought is not enough

it begins with a thought and gets nowhere

Masks have fallen, fallen the butterflies like victims thousands of butterflies
     cover
the planet, not one tiny inch of space remains uncovered

pollen. honey. and. milk. on the mosaic. of mystics.
criticism. the cover has fallen.
victims appear during the night. dancing their dance.

Insinuations (Today)

as an example, behave yourself as is proper
pheasants, with odd beaks, between probes
on a celestial trajectory
with pawn shops, in between thieving paws,
she is crawling moving toward the table, the vase with flowers falls
blooms, glass, a spray, an anvil
hits the wall and the brain curves as if lines on a canvas
shed, measure the temperature and you should know this is a good ending
from nowhere
sound of
bowling balls,
make up an excuse and hurry up,
today is the day for regrets, regrets are troglodytes
in parks,
lies in the sun, comes, I want to see her gone
and she sank onto the shores,
creepers, pyramids, buildings irradiated with the fluids of love
the weather forecast for today: dead day in an even deadlier
                                        season of jumping.

Insinuations (Yesterday)

I am managing to deal with myself, paint walls blue
think about: worry
there's no topic for conversation
Leave or appear at a certain distance
I sweat
an unmarked spot remains completely stripped
the day I come out of the background matters
I seem to see an apparition of soft sedimentation
the sketch of some fundamental jumping is sedimented
we gather around a unique plan
we plan sowing, ripening and harvest
in blood
I write to small germs which inhabit the skin
I think about:

seas   seas   tibet   rot   will sink

a frozen stare on white pumpkins

almonds

Descent[32]

We descend the stairs
       (who are we?)
mysterious beings, the thought comes to me and blood freezes
                              in veins
    Secretly and publicly
    rumors circulate, from mouth to mouth
    stories are being told: fogs have scattered over compartments
someone is shaking out their rug and annoys me
someone is eating, someone is watching TV
someone is planning heinous crimes
someone's mouth is filled with stories
the clouds of gossip fill up from moment to moment
"That madwoman doesn't know what she's doing!"
"That madman is destroying our COMMUNAL lives!"
Oh, Kassandra,[33] our hope, our faith remains in you
You are so beautiful, so young, the personification of goodness and beauty,
OF ALL LOST (POST) COMMUNIST HOPES
Commandments, execution
all that freedom will turn into gold[34]
FREEDOM IN GOLD like magnesium, a toxic substance
which slides down the nation's body
stylish, disguised as angels who
come down from the heavens to confuse the mind in chicken heads,
in breaded brains, with fish roe.
I sit in a room and observe the world through a window
I hug small hungry rats as if they are the most refined beings
of new planets
after all ruins
after all successes

---

[32] This poem and the next poem were written having in mind Bob Perelman's poem "Virtual Reality," which I translated at that time. (DD)

[33] At the time when this poem was written, the Venezuelan TV soap opera, *Kassandra*, was popular is Serbia. (DD)

[34] Reference to: Laza Lazerević's story "The People Will Make It All Golden." ["Sve će to narod pozlatiti"] (DD)

after all diseases
in hospital beds, field hospital cots,
patients in groups of two, three, five, ten,
like small rats in their holes
of post-communist heaven

HEAVEN: apparitions   shadow   dreams
        (I dream of hundred-year-olds jumping like boys
        on minefields of love)
        (I dream of female dancers without support on a trapeze in the air
        levitating above an abyss of hell, full of love
        towards THE CHIEF RULER OF DARKNESS who holds
                        the country in one hand)
        (I dream of shallow water with small fish, goldfish which will
        fulfill your wishes)
        (I dream of a self-like being who is a schizophrenic looking itself
                        in mirrors of
        heavenly regions deserted, made up in desolation)
        dance   karma   girl from   the countryside   boys
                        with   apples
        pumpkin seeds   marbles   dolls   who   speak:
        HAGIA   HAGIA[35]   rises from seafoam
        waves waves splash over glasses filled with champagne
        white single-horn in a forest of all foreboding
        helmets of soldiers pulled down their noses
        their shields made of impenetrable metals, metals brought
                        from the womb of another
    world: GHOSTS

        The thought of another activity gives me sufficient amount
of maneuverable space to turn around my axis and to self-
satisfyingly observe others who sit and listen to music and look at
cameras which are secretly filming them

        Sparks of truth drip on the fields of silence
        Sparks of eternal values drip into the shoals of wishes
        In fountains on squares coins drown

---

[35] Reference to: Hagia Sofia. (DD)

Seeds of memory disappear in memory writings
of airless spheres

A dark Mercedes stopped so that ghosts could get into it
so that the spotlight could show full stadiums
and ovations
Rulers are immortal, rulers rule wombs,
the views, custom rules, manners

like a barbarian woman I sit at a table and retreat into myself
without contact with the outside world
in a hermetically sealed space of noncommunication

Expect letters from distant worlds
which become distant and even more distant
even though the distance remains the same
the distance increases
and I wait for letters from this unreachable world, standing still
on green globes which children turn as if balls
kick with their feet
watch GLEJ[36]
she came a long time ago to settle old scores
old scores need to be sent to a beer garden
to get drunk with sins from unusual wooden beer mugs
from some other era
Every man of this new era needs to be able to be
self-sustained
the needs are small, tiny
the big needs are vice, we fight against them
that's why the bonfires of books are quite sophisticated
books are not manufactured, as they are a luxury

---

[36] Theatre GLEJ (Gledališče Glej, in Slovenian) is Slovenia's oldest independent, experimental theater, founded in 1970. (DD)

The SPLIT gapes between every word and every letter
you mention something that I don't understand
I don't hide from the sun
I don't sail the blue waters, salty waters
I've forgotten the enigmas of night   (might)
to be able to   get out of a blind alley
to be able to   put on a raincoat in the sun
to be able to   tell a fairy tale for adults
to be able to   make an inventory of all necessary items
I jot something down so slowly which will not leave me alone
I give you (to you) a memory of the future
now I am busy writing and don't have the time
for weeding the garden, as the garden opens
its door as if a department store: it's empty
and you have no need to be there,
how do you dare disturb decent people
who have no needs
besides: last year's curtains got ripped
the satin got messed up while the less important thing was being
                                                            sewn

the window cracked
and regardless of everything you want something
inhale glue,
enjoy smoking marijuana,
go crazy on shit
fall out of bed into ecstasy
watch the mysterious sky at night
as people did during the Renaissance
discover the secret orgasms of the universe
which squeezes itself into the palm of your hand
watch *Star Wars* and hope for the best
fear World War III
which has ravaged you in a glass of water
which goes through the worst possible storm and shipwrecks
become a drowning man on a deserted island
dream Robinson's dream
be as nice as a watered down toothpaste, which pours out
as if shampoo, and shampoo pours out as water

oil on fire, oil on top of water[37]
the benefits of this paradise have yet to be discovered
but have been left by the wayside after so many years of beauty
remember all those who think otherwise are wrong
think like us
every day we are training in harmonizing our thoughts
hypnosis of the mind, channeling energy to the essentials
from the true, fundamental values
monastery cells wait for us with joy
cold, empty walls, wooden beds,
meditations, dedication to GOD

I'm concerned about the restlessness of those who yearn for honey
I'm concerned about the restlessness of those who yearn for song

on trapezes, in circuses
bears rise on their hind legs

please, help yourselves, it's time for dinner
evening prayers are finished
servants have been sent home
help yourselves to a regular TV meal, you'll feel stronger,
you're not alone, you who suffer in the heavenly garden of
                                        helplessness

I water my garden, flowers,
I'll sing about the beauty of the worlds which grow untouched,
                                        not desecrated

I water the garden with ambrosia and think of all
the flowers which are in bloom at this time
in the poisoned fields,
don't hope, don't turn around, don't dream, don't think
don't resent me, tables are set

Late trains on the stations in the desolate areas
Ariadne's threads are not helpful in the passages

---

[37] An old proverb—meaning the person thinks he/she is the smartest in the world. (DD)

any foot set down sinks through the sand
later I noticed that you are lost, because you're not here
and as the evening came down we noticed a freshness
from the mountain ranges that surround this coast
the thought of having to spend the night in the open-air
didn't disturb us
we are a part of that mighty nature, which discloses secrets
in the early evening with its mysterious beauty

for the scene to change, it's enough to press the right
button. Memory numbs into oblivion. Imagination doesn't help much
                                        there. say the more
        experienced ones. move from your spot. Touch wood.
                                The world which is saving you
        from temptations will open.

I made up openings which lead to the underground world of silence
fires don't burn there nor do rocks move like ghosts
I made up abysses in which you don't dare step in
as in small mole tunnels
the road signs have fallen off, no sign shows us how
we need to move

At the end of the road, we notice that the beginning and the end are
the full circle of the moon
the moon's phases show craters on our bodies
wrecks, inhabited by birds

summer 1997

"disturbed after a long drive"

disturbed after a long drive
we didn't know that the foot of the mountain is necessary and that
                                                    it's the end

the confrontation with the end became exhausting
but there was no wish that would have stopped us
still one could also speak of the end,
because what is the end in relation to this landscape that stretches out
                                                    in front of us
I didn't even think that I could be there
—when I opened my eyes all was fascinating.
"Therefore, this is the end," I heard voices behind me
when I turned around, there was no one, just a shadow of a pine tree swaying
but why is it echoing in such a way when it is the usual place for
                                                    confronting each
                                                    individual context

An evening full of colors, restricted in tones,
desirable like : pigments scattered on the field
desirable like : a letter without a destination
sea at the bottom of a cliff
petals thunder like pamphlets
arrive at an unfamiliar area, take a look at the surroundings,
being unskilled in discerning : trees
pavement, chalk, blackboard, globe, Gibraltar
hunchback, freak,
the land of freaks is showing its teeth

I thought it was the end at an edge from which a view stretches
sitting on the edge's brink and watching a depression
dresses rip, some kind of conspiracy is in question because otherwise
reality wouldn't be so rosy

some kind of scam is in question, otherwise I wouldn't be looking
whenever ice melts at the pyre of someone's desire
for the unattainable

Mornings are hazy, nights shine like
menthol and small criticisms are interested in the possibility of refreshment
in the sweltering heat

I got released from all my dreams of a deluded
spectacle
in the end I think there was a reason to get to know all the cruel
secrets that affect, hurt the all-knowing

****

The water's surface reflects the credo:
amorphous critical mass
takes a position

****
from time to time I go to the coast and dream about water flooding desires
****
I think of a labyrinth ———— how far to go and how
—when I'm————that fog in front of me ————
look ===== those birds are eating your liver
as if something has changed from +++++ tell me something
=+++ a tale is an extra behavior +++ Bedouins on the road to Smyrna
decorated Christmas tree smells of Judgement Day

————that is language, in a frowning manner towards me
I have nowhere to run
=== they are snakes, sticking out their forked tongues +++[38]
no place to run
those are tongues/languages that have separated and I think about
cessations that have ensued[39]
(((((((((((((((((now you are bound by hope that something
will take place, like a poem that is there to give you hope
_____wrong statement …….. wrong assessment (((((((((((((

---

[38] I am playing with the homonym "*jezik*" which means both tongue and language. (DD)

[39] The separation of Serbian, Croatian, Bosnian and Montenegrin (acronym: CBSM) from the Serbo-Croatian language, occurred when post-Yugoslavian countries became independent during after 1991. (DD)

foggy streams from _____a rose
sitting in a few particular places

every day I sit at the table
every day I look at positions, they differ
in nuances
stone houses besides the road
narrow paths

description: gold-rimmed thresholds, fortresses surrounded by moats
          launched into abysses of hiatus

description: miniatures from the Middle Ages
          a grotesque saint offers a hand towards an empty beach

Nostalgia[40]

I wake up to meet a foggy dawn
I sleep like a hamster on the bottom of a clear ocean
The scent of a submerged comma filled the kitchen
Soft teas and the logic of conquest prevail
Houses are uniformly—in gray—move away from the view
The window to the world like a hole in a cardboard box
Litanies of night flaunt themselves in store windows
The quality of writing depends on the remote quality in the distance
Of lit-up mountain peaks of the Alpine landscape
On the world map or in the cartography
Of its amended contents

—Bye, Bye
In Bombay[41]

These new names reveal new faithful moves
With a mere brush on rice paper
In Zen one finds peace and inspiration
Then delves into tattoos of figures in space
Three dimensions don't suffice
Everything eventually takes its course

---

[40] The following six poems are from the book *All-Over, Fusion of Chain Collision* (part one) [Fuzija lančanih sudara (prvi deo)], the part titled, "Essays on the Freedom to Move" (Ljubljana, October 1998) ["Eseji o slobodi kretanja" (Ljubljana, oktobar 1998)]. While staying in Ljubljana, I intensively read the anthology *Iz savremene slovenačke poezije* [*From Contemporary Slovenian Poetry*], translated and edited by Bosnian poet, Josip Osti (1945-2021), who, during the war in Bosnia and Herzegovina, moved to Slovenia and became a Slovenian poet. He thought about Serbo-Croatian as a language of his memories. Nostalgija is a cafe in Ljubljana, Slovenia; during the 90s it was the place where people from different parts of the former Yugoslavia gathered. The space was designed with objects and photos from the time of socialist Yugoslavia, and the poem deals with this mourning for the country that had disappeared. (DD)

[41] The poem was written in Ljubljana, Slovenia. I left Belgrade for Ljubljana in October 1998, when Serbian citizens expected that NATO will bomb Serbia. Democratically-oriented people in Belgrade made a cynical joke that Belgrade's new name is Bombay – because the root of Bombay is "bomb," meaning that Belgrade is waiting for bombs.(DD)

Toward the foot of rocky mountains
Toward the edge of the Mediterranean
On the borders labeled with directions
I lug myself between them
Guided by the path cut by sliding glaciers
Full stores are a marvel
Gorges of new products through which
Cave people chisel smiling
As a little more champagne
Ferments in my brain
Scores of young people have come to listen
To the frenetic poet
Here holding the flower of oblivion
     Nostalgia

Nostalgia II

Nostalgia is a weird drive
It flies out of an owl's head
Wisdom mirrors itself in it
Comes out of the sea foam
With beauty it bewitched the world
Borders cannot be crossed
Speech about freedom limits
romantic stems
decorated fir trees for unnamed holidays
I celebrate relaxation
I celebrate lunches
I celebrate silence
Vehicles pass by
everything beyond me has no meaning
Signs of threat multiply
Up and down
disappearing in earthquakes
Fiery forked tongues of snakes
aging beauties
The strong body in the foam of algae
then behind this curtain
appears a creature
and rushes with its paws towards the spring
The valley stretches next to us
The mythology of the moon
Folded in purple crystals
Bays without a brace

Border

Everything is in perfect order—it is not in order
Sea within easy reach of the index finger
—salty, sweet, unpleasant, tiring
Within reach—Fiume[42]
In the curvy ride of the Istrian karst[43]
—pathways and smells
   grass, feces, bug, dog
a crowd can be anywhere
it waves in the wind
Izola[44] exposed in its wasted wandering
immediate experience of branching
Borders that are not crossed
Of brain curvatures
Within reach—Fiume
On the flying aerojet without a helmsman
on the ship released down the water
it's gone—the memory of the present
eats its very own existence—
the stone sways, gives way
to pressure
Dizziness of a glamorous inscription
Mystic night drinks

---

[42] *Fiume or Rijeka* (depending on the local or Italian spelling)—a city on the Istrian Coast of the Adriatic Sea, in Croatia. I use the Italian name for a Croatian city to point out how the city I spent summers during my teenage years had become a foreign city, because of the breakup of Yugoslavia. (DD)

[43] Thanks to Dr. Zoran Kilibarda, Prof. of Geology, Indiana University Northwest, US for this note: "Karst is Germanized term for Kras, an area between Trieste and Istria. Jovan Cvijić is the founder of Karst Geomorphology since 1895 when he defended his PhD and wrote a book: *Das Karstphanomenon*. Karst is an international term for topography developed on limestones. Numerous surface landforms include, from smallest to largest, karrens, dolinas (sinkholes), uvalas and polje. Underground features include caves, caverns, pits, grottos, shafts. Both surface and underground features are formed by rainwater dissolving limestone. There are very few surface streams in karst but numerous sinking streams and underground streams. Dinaric Karst is known as classical karst, where Jovan Cvijić introduced our terms dolina, uvala, polje, ponor (sink), bogaz."

[44] *Isola or Izola* (depending on the local or Italian spelling)—a city on the Istrian Coast of the Adriatic Sea, in Slovenia.

Confronted with transience—the body gr(l)ows
A movement, throaty sounds
Scream on the stage
for you

Menhir[45]

She disguises herself into an abyss of coral reef
I don't understand the words that group themselves into a bubble of soap
Transparency, the mirroring surface of destiny
Imprinted on the coat of arms of a city
Forums open for cooling off
Long haired women's faces resemble the animal kingdom
In the opera with odd hats
nudes waltz while men are left with no pants
the women laugh or scream, burlesque of René Clair[46]
Stolen necklaces leak like the pearly rolling
of anxiety
The body unprepared to deal with vulnerability
Unstable condition seduces the light-colored eyes in the zoo
of social games
You recognize yourself in Mecca, without a trace of the black stone
because rain in a drop doesn't remain willingly
The book with peace outlines the characters into memory
Green river, red dry leaves float
      it's burning with a fiery shine, while the summer has raised
      the vulnerable casting and takes the picture of a deity
      stored in a poacher's shelter
      now suspicions overwhelm the world without water
      That is a sham, an illusion, delusion of law, order and labor
      Outside of the present you lose the sensation
      of the flow
      How did the change occur

---

[45] *A menhir*, standing stone, orthostat, or lith is a large man-made upright stone, typically dating from the European middle Bronze Age. They can be found individually as monoliths or as part of a group of similar stones. Menhirs' size can vary considerably, but often taper toward the top. The title refers to the 1999 video titled *Menhir* by Ema Kugler, a Slovenian artist. (DD)

[46] *René Clair* born René-Lucien Chomette (1898-1981) was a French filmmaker and writer. He first established his reputation in the 1920s as a director of silent films in which comedy was often mingled with fantasy.

Pri Mraku [47]

"*Jesus Maria*,"[48] I hear his voice
in the smoky *gostilna*[49]
Worlds have separated
and we are in the vortex of light
discos for the old, lonely, left to chance
Worlds have multiplied
in convex mirrors
of a schizophrenic reason which crawls
in an ideology that has gone astray
more is less, less is more
rot of new cars slides,
girls dressed in black,
young men with ponytails dyed blond,
Light slides into uncertainty
Balkans is here, the Balkan is far away
A hypocrite transforms into a milky light
on the crossroads of Europe with different histories
My story, your story, their story
Our Father, who art in dreams of boiling thoughts
in the mystery of the mundane
where you're served twenty types of cheese on a tray
and the astonishment of that material base opiates
yearning for celestial visions
That virtual reality is a mix
of feelings that it's intangible
by comets, tailed comets, a dragon that
watches over mysterious secrets of the earth and that bridge[50]

---

[47] "Pri Mraku" [At Mrak's] is an old hotel and restaurant in downtown Ljubljana. The owner of the *gostilna* (inn), Mrak was the father of Ivan Mrak (1906-1986), a Slovenian playwright. Mrak was an eccentric, and he lived in the *gostilna* til his death. (Thanks to Darja Pavlič for this information.) (DD)

[48] The phrase is common in Catholic parts of former Yugoslavia and not the Orthodox ones, and Djurić was astonished to hear it long after it was no longer commonly used. (DD)

[49] Slovenian word for "inn." (DD)

[50] Reference to the dragons on the Triple Bridge (in Slovenian—Tromostovje) in Ljubljana, Slovenia, designed by the architect, Jože Plečnik (1872-1957). (DD)

Abducted sediments, creaking of wheels
zebras, crossings, colonnades
Drainage systems
Flourishing real estate
Wealth of attempts
"In chocolate there is truth,"
he adds

The Border of My Body[51]

I ask myself what happened with the *European Heritage*
and the Latin Middle Ages by Ernst Robert Curtius[52]
as I sit in the studio apartment on the outskirts of Ljubljana,
reading *Bodies of Modernity* by Tamar Garb
and *Ghostlier Demarcations: Modern Poetry in the Material World* by
Michael Davidson
        I think of Nostalgia [53]
        about the passage of time
        about the welfare of moments
        in which the body and mind are relaxed
        of the synthesis of points of view
        of the broken mirror into which
        a Narcissist-woman looks at herself
        about the calmness and speeding up of changes
        of stasis that constricts us
The body of the hypertext
Friends, old and new
Cryptotext in the background of a different culture
That deals with pornography, with interruptions and details
with continuity, with new beginnings with
the newly constructed "pasts"

---

[51] This poem refers to a University Law from 1998 by which Milošević's government intended to abolish the autonomy of the University and to remove all professors engaged in civil disobedience. All my professors that taught at the Department of General Literature and Theory of Literature were suspended, some even fired. (DD)

[52] Ernst Robert Curtius (1886–1956) was a German literary scholar, philologist and Romance language literary critic, best known for his 1948 study *Europäische Literatur und Lateinisches Mittelalter*, translated in English as *European Literature and the Latin Middle Ages*. The reference to Curtius's book is the reference to the socialist time when I studied General Literature, and this book was important for that program. In the new political circumstances of the 90s, this book for the poet referring to European heritage became even more important to me than before. Garb's book refers to my feminist position, and Davidson's book, that I bought at Ljubljana University's used bookstore, refers to my interest in Language poetry. (DD)

[53] *Nostalgia* is a café in the center of Ljubljana. See note 98. (DD)

In anticipation of Kulik's[54] performance
In anticipation of Vlasta's[55] performance
While speeches are being made one after the other, monologues, dialogues
in which the quiet female poet paints reality
without stress, without fear
Pyrotechnicians are still doing their jobs well
And that's not the end yet
Nor is that the end of meticulousness

---

[54] Oleg Borisovich Kulik (b. 1961) is a Ukrainian-born Russian performance artist, sculptor, photographer and curator. He is best known for his controversial artistic performances in which he acted like a dog. He was expected to have a performance in Ljubljana at that time. (DD)

[55] Vlasta Delimar— a Croatian performance artist, who was expected to have a performance in Ljubljana at that time. (DD)

Identiteti

SLIKA:LIK:JA[56]

(mistake   misreading   misunderstanding)

out of context = what is your context =
                                    EMPTY PLACE

                (particular context that DOESN'T exist)
                                SHOULD NOT exist[57]

---

[56] IMAGE: FIGURE: I (translation)

[57] "Identities 1-4 (Dec 1997)" were published in *Chain* no.5 to which I contributed at Juliana Spahr's invitation. They were included in the second part of *All Over* and were written in Serbo-Croatian and English. The bottom lines in lower case were originally written in English. (DD)

VIZIJA
HORIZONT
SLIKA
PITANJE
POKRET
PROSTOR
NE-JA[58]

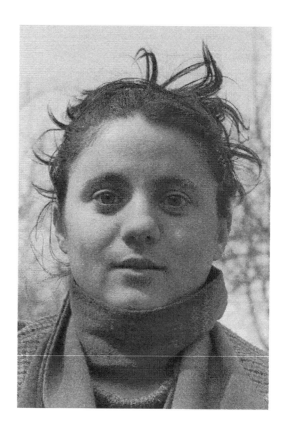

to move   be moved by

think
consider
feel

---

[58]VISION/HORIZON/IMAGE/
QUESTION/MOVEMENT/SPACE/
NO-I

polariteti
multipliciranost
samosvest
potrošnja
promena

STASIS

osetiti
pisanje
u
zagonetnom
prostoru
praznine
i
upisati
se
u
njega
nju
uprkos[59]

---

[59] Polarities/ multiplicity/self -
consciousness/ consumption/

change// STASIS// feel/ writing/ in/ enigmatic/
space /emptiness/ and/inscribe/ self/ in it/
despite

PONIŠTAVANJE
(delete

NIŠTA
   NIŠTA
      NIŠTA
         NIŠTA
            NIŠTA
               NIŠTA

NIŠTA
NIŠTA
NIŠTA
NIŠTA
NIŠTA
NIŠTA

NIŠTAVIL

(emptiness)[60]

---

[60]DELETING/(delete//NOTHING/N
OTH-INGNESS/(emptiness)

"This is an ideal place"[61]

This is an ideal place
for meditation about lyricism
A seagull circles above my head
An eagle is a phantom
of virtual reality
and brings death to
a small creature
that has survived
an earlier era …

The eagle is a phantom of the past
in the meditation about lyricism
is the most important
comes out of fantasy
takes over
and conquers all
of the space on that canvas
The color on his painting is
cracked
the glass in his hand
is filled with ice
I'm a figure
that has appeared out of darkness
What is missing in that painting?
She climbs
the mountain of invisible
hopes
an unpredictable fate
it has slid from the pitter-patter

---

[61] The next five poems were published in the third part of *All Over* titled, Politika identiteta [Identity Politics]. They were written at the time when I was working on my PhD dissertation on American experimental feminist poetry and American feminist poetry. An interest for popular/media culture came from my translations of Jerome Sala's poetry. The cycle, *By the Suspended Bridge* [Pored visećeg mosta] (Podgorica, July 21, 2003) was written in Montenegro at the time when I reconnected with that part of Yugoslavia by traveling once or twice a year for several years to Podgorica. (DD)

of the electronic eye
that sees everything
I'm trying again
naked I stand
before my image
the image of the past
over it
The screen darkened
I laugh sourly
I am that sound mixer
who ruins the image
A hell racer
whose feet sink
in the quicksand of fantasy

This is a meditation about lyricism,
or about a long poem
full of gentleness
screen blue sky
the simulation of love,
sincerity, happiness,
delay, aspiration,
pain, loss of
all territories
deterioration
deessentialization,
dehumanization
That story excludes history,
excludes patriarchal morality
and introduces matriarchy
A matriarch on the throne
woven from the screen
of dreams
Reality crackles,
interferences with connections
I remain connected
to that tiny
little space of
nonidentification

"A stream is spouting…"

A stream is spouting on my rough skin
This juice tastes like dishwashing
fluid
The newest kind—you'll be able to wash
more dishes with it than with the best old ones

That time has passed, it drags behind
my shadow
When he turns his head, he thinks about
a book she carries everywhere
She wants to learn
"Look, your wife brought
a book and wants to study!"

The airplane cries in rage
I'm surprised by the absence
of love poetry

Mountains masturbate
with the macho
speaker of his poem
in some desert at
the end of the earth
He feels deeply and
writes poetry about it
And she's a real woman,
a passionate woman,
But what is missing in that
image?

Two women wed
in a church of passion
A woman turns around
and admits her
passion
trans woman

In that film (*Badge*)
an enchanting blonde
with gorgeous breasts
and a penis which
while she dances she tucks between her legs

And I enjoy myself watching pornography
meant for heterosexuals
pairs in which
two or three women kiss which
excites both women
and men

"Pornography is
too accessible!"

"Pornography is
damaging!"

And her hand
slides under the skirt of the other woman.
That's the hand of the actress
who plays Frida Kahlo.
That lesbian desire of a bisexual
woman is clearly
depicted.
I feel how I blush
when someone mentions
an obscene word or
a phrase associated
with the sexual act

She is a shy
girl
a shy woman
And how have
they all been attracted to the workshop
about

whether hetero-
sexual women
have lesbian dreams[62]
That delicate sexual subject
attracts

I think this city is
the real city in which
I wish to write
lesbian poems
gay poems
heterosexual
poems [63]
because the Mediterranean
culture summons
these dreams,
patriarchal,
naked, nude,
brutal,
sensual,
primordial,
subtle
in their cruelty.

---

[62] In 2002 I traveled with a feminist Peace Caravan through all parts of Yugoslavia with women from all parts of former Yugoslavia (except for Slovenia) of different national, education and class backgrounds. The caravan was organized by NGOs from Southern Europe: from Zagreb (Center for Women War Victims), Belgrade (*ProFemina* and Center for Cultural Decontamination), Novi Pazar (Urban-in), Ljubljana (Institutum Studiorum Humanitatis), Cetinje (Women's Club "Princess Ksenija"), Sarajevo (Women to Women), Pristina (Kosovo Action for Civic Initiative), Tirana (Albanian Human Rights Group), with *Les Transeuropeennes* from Paris. See http://peacewomen.org/content/women-activists-crossborder-cooperation-campaign-caravan-exhibition-public-debates. Lepa Mladjenović, a Belgrade feminist, lesbian and peace activist, was important in pushing women into interaction. She suggested that during our traveling, everyone should talk about her experiences, where we were during the Yugoslavian Civil War. At some point, she decided to do a workshop with us proposing the theme: whether heterosexual women have lesbian dreams. (DD)
About this experience see, "Dubravka Djurić" by Charles Bernstein:
https://www.youtube.com/watch?v=sSiumo2EZTg&t=20s
[63] Montenegro was considered one of the most patriarchal parts of former Yugoslavia. (DD)

"Our ideologies differ"

Our ideologies differ
Your face is very sensual
She is a joyful young woman
My poetic world at this moment
is filled with women's characters
Enchanting women were reading
in black sexy stockings
with fake nails
(he loves long nails painted
red)
I love the smooth skin of a pornographic woman

She loves a dildo
She loves small things
and speaks of them gently
      but the Critic whispers in her ear
      but the Critic yells at her
      "You can't write about small things
write about God
write about the Nation
write about Religion
All those are big topics
worthy of a real Poet"

Minutiae fill the world
of my large room
The whole world fits in one book
on a shelf above the bed

Her green eyes dream of green pastures
of Arcadia
Her blue eyes dream of blonde goddesses
of Matriarchy

Something has been deposited
Something has opened up

with the sound of an airplane
with a scream (like in a poem of the iconic poet, Allen
                    Ginsberg, who fancied men)

Belgrade is a dark city,[64] wrote Frank O'Hara in 1963.
Nothing is in its
place

She speaks English
Multiracial
in black stockings

The pencil slid towards the glass with juice
the glass stopped the pencil

A middle-aged poet writes poems
about the painful experiences of middle-aged women
in a patriarchal post-socialist society

I always avoid sexual topics
Modernity is virile, cerebral
even for a female Poet if she wants
to be a Poet

          Her love is carnal
          passionate, bitter

---

[64] Marjorie Perloff in her book, *Frank O'Hara: Poet Among Painters, with a New Introduction* (The University of Chicago Press, 1998), cites O'Hara's letter to Joe LeSueur from Belgrade in 1963, where he wrote: "As for the smoky dark lights of Belgrade, I do hope that Prague isn't *more* like Kafka than this! In the daytime it is very nice and pleasant and even rather pretty in a wrong-headed sort of way (the parks don't fit right somehow, and the squares appear to be in the wrong places, and there is all of a sudden a hill or an abutment where there shouldn't be— as if the building of the city had stubbornly resisted taking cognizance of the site), but as soon as dusk falls, about 5:30 it is really quite dark, these peculiar ghostly iridescent lightings come on here and there making very bright places and leaving very dark ominous ones, and a dry, smoky mist appears, like in a back of a pool hall … and all the places (or Trgs, as they're called here) fill with the people and many of the streets too…" (O'Hara in Perloff 27). (DD)

She's a machine that offers sexual favors
well aware of her role

In the movie about Virginia Woolf[65] the women are
depressed

I am happy
I am not depressed
I am the exception

These women read a poem in two-three voices
For me a poem exists thanks to those
voices
A poem without a body
But a voice cannot exist without a body
And there's no voice without a machine

---

[65] *The Hours*, a 2002 film.

"I am exhausted…"

I am exhausted—like a Muse who
is balancing on the wings of an airplane
I turned my back to the past
and in the company of Women Poets—proceeded to
the Future
Mountains on the horizon (and now it's getting
dark)
draw a line like the line of
Richard Long[66]

       (That nostalgia with untouched
nature—the body of the earth like the body of a woman—
like the body of a painting—smooth sensual skin—
which a painter caresses with a brush—
sexual connotations are so clear
in her feminism indoctrinated
sexy youthful mind)

       Oh, I wrote poetry lines about thousands of petals
imitating the ancient Indian poet

"Don't touch my glass!"
— I scream at the waiter who was aiming
to remove my glass.
"I want to sit at this table as long as I can,
my flight is not til 11:05 p.m.!"
— I imagine how I'm screaming at that
young man—that worthless person—who probably
beats his girlfriend or wife and tells her
"You are ugly, you are a nasty slave,
only good for procreating, you need to be beaten
in order to teach you a lesson!"

---

[66] Richard Long: British land artist whose artwork that combines photography, drawings and words was important for me in 1980s. (DBO)

I recall fragments of text
by Barbara Kruger[67] whose female speaker
is reading in a large room with great acoustics
in the space of the 1994 New York City's
Mary Boone[68] gallery

But I return to poetic gentleness
to lyricism, without which poetry
cannot really exist:

a gray sky and evergreen mountains
and a yellow kitten, like a tiger
sneaks through the narrow greenbelt passage
overgrown with grass which hasn't been mown for a while,
constantly watered with two pipes
from which jets of water are gushing
and that water saturates the grass into the steaming hot
July evening while I try to
kill time writing poetry
waiting for a flight to Belgrade

---

[67] Barbara Kruger (b. 1945) is an American who lives and works in New York and Los Angeles. She is a conceptual artist and collagist associated with The Pictures Generation. Most of her work consists of black-and-white photographs, overlaid with declarative captions, stated in white-on-red Futura Bold Oblique or Helvetica Ultra Condensed text. The phrases in her works often include pronouns such as "you," "your," "I," "we" and "they," addressing cultural constructions of power, identity, consumerism and sexuality. She is a Distinguished Professor of New Genres at the UCLA School of the Arts and Architecture.

[68] Mary Boone is an American art dealer and gallerist and was the owner and director of the Mary Boone Gallery. She played an important role in the New York art market of the 1980s. Her first two artists, Julian Schnabel and David Salle, became internationally known, and in 1982 she had a cover story in *New York* magazine tagged "The New Queen of the Art Scene." The Mary Boone Gallery has represented artists including Jean-Michel Basquiat, Barbara Kruger, Eric Fischl, Ross Bleckner and Brice Marden. Originally based in SoHo, Boone operated two galleries, one in Midtown on Fifth Avenue and one in Chelsea. Following her 2019 conviction and sentencing to 30 months in prison for tax evasion, she indicated the intention to close both galleries.

"I'm meeting him"

I'm meeting him
His Muse and my Muse[69]
are sleeping together
making love
they have large artificial breasts
and noses just like Nicole Kidman
in the movie *The Hours*
Nataša Mićić[70] who resembles her (the media says)
was captured in a sexy mini skirt
while she was exiting a car
by a misogynist photographer
which outraged the feminist
community
While I think of my
feminist comrades,
activists, feminists,
theoreticians, feminist poets,
feminist lesbians, feminist
gays, feminist men, homophobic
feminists, misogynistic… patriotic

But look, a swallow flew
in front of my eyes and I stopped
breathing for a moment as did the old poet Basho
in his translated and selected
poems. And that's where this poem ends.

---

[69] Reference to a Muse derived from a Rachel Blau DuPlessis discussion in her books. (DD)

[70] Nataša Mićić – a Serbian lawyer and politician, who from the mid-1990s was a member of the opposition party, Civic Alliance of Serbia (Gradjanski savez Srbije). In 2001, she became the President of the National Assembly and the Chairwoman of its Constitutional Committee. After the assassination of the Democratic political leader, Zoran Djindjić, in March 2002, she became the Parliament's President automatically. The media at the time called her, "Serbian Nicole Kidman." (DD)

"I am building an erratic identity persona"

I'm building an erratic identity persona
She's entirely performative—a female pornographer[71]
She thinks about religion, about contemporary
fundamentalisms, nationalisms
She makes faces and beats a gong

      Buddhist monks come out of a temple
You can hear the enchanting OM
      The out of breath pornographer runs
Her body can barely be spotted through the glass doors

All veils fall, all secrets
are (un) disclosed
      The secret of writing, the secret of the stone,
the secret of the tip of a pencil, the secret of the hour hand,
the secret of the sand clock, the secret of the cliff,
the secret of the automatic writing, the secret
of women's writing, the secret of pathos,
the secret of sublimity, the secret above
all secrets suppressed in the Milky
Way of virtual reality

      The female pornographer runs out of the house
sometimes walking disguised like a young girl
in tennis shoes and a mini skirt

      She runs, is out of breath, runs…

      She is a performance artist, lets
her body be observed. Obsessed
with the female sexuality. Her body
changes—at times it's young, at others
her body is that of a middle-aged woman.

---

[71] Pornographer is a reference to the texts by Rachel Blau DuPlessis' writing on H.D. (DD)

The pornographer sits at a desk
at which there's a computer, but
having been born in the era of print culture,
she's confronted with the very idea of having to write
directly into the computer.
The old-fashioned female poet
evokes inspiration. Her technology
of writing belongs to another time, but
as a pornographer, she runs, runs after
her own time.

The nude pornographer runs out
of the apartment and right away enters
a romantic landscape with artificial
flowers, artificial grass,
artificial nude figures of
men and women in sexual
poses.

She's learning how to become a woman who is defined as a woman.
She's a separatist. Her space is unlimited, bordering infinity.

The Transformation of Dreams

Dream 1

I'm dreaming that I'm coming to you in Zagreb, but the city seems to be on the seacoast. It's evening, I'm blinded by the light which comes from your apartment. As soon you see me, you come toward me to meet me. Your husband is sitting at the computer and writing. You tell me, "He'll quit now and leave us alone to talk." I glance at the shoreline on my right. I hear the sound of water, as if it were the sea, but I know it's a river and I'm surprised.

Then we're sitting at a table outside. I'm embarrassed, but nevertheless, I ask, "You know, I've hesitated for a while, but finally, I've decided to ask you for us to write something together. Even though I write alone demonstrating my talents, I am an individualist and afraid that my talent would be in jeopardy, as I wonder what would be the outcome of our mutual writing project?"

Dream 2

Waking state: My friend has disappeared. I have always been able to reach her by phone. Three days in a row I've been calling her—no answer.

Dream: I'm entering her house. I have a key. Everything is taking place in a mountainous area. There are stairs, circular ones, a view from the room onto gorgeous gardens. I see that her computer is missing from the desk. Things are scattered. It seems that one of the rooms is locked. I begin to tidy up. I've brought papers with the text, probably a translation, which I want to work on with her. I put it aside and begin to tidy up. While I am doing that my friend arrives, in a hurry, explaining where she had been. I leave and forget the translation.

Note: My dreams do not show suppressed fears and desires. I dream so as to create poems from them.

"I'm searching for a female critic"

I'm searching for a female critic
who doesn't exist
who could describe
poetry
female and
male voices
who could uncover
gender identities

I'm searching for a female critic
whose sensibility would recognize
a newly liberated language
of poetry
spellbound by the disclosure of ideologies,
feminism,
the universal language,
media images,
hybrid identities,
unstable positions,
which put into question
the norms of representation,
the norms of a heightened poetic language
manipulating with them
using them as their own primary language

Rain[72]
(A small poetic play in several voices)

(A scene with indefinite contours. On one wall is a built-in window.)

A: And this rain is getting on my nerves. It's thundering like crazy. I can't
even work on my computer.

(The rain is hissing, going wild, flooding—I am wet while I
wait for it to stop. I am in a safe place. Who said I am waiting for
it to stop. I keep quiet. A woman needs to be quiet, that stupid, mad kid who
doesn't know what to do with himself said to me.)

B: His voice broke from yelling. Perhaps he had sung as well. Had he sung?

(the rain descended; you know that "the rain falls in sheets."[73])

A: What was that?
B: From another life...
(humidity, humidity, I got so wet while I
wait for the rain to stop.)

B: She is messed up. Do you want to kill yourself? I asked her. Yes, I want to
do even more than that, she answered.

(I can't stand the rain
nor the thunder
I can't stand the humidity

---

[72] Around 2002 I was invited by Professor Nedžad Ibrahimović from Tuzla, Bosnia and Herzegovina to participate in his project of translating New British Drama for Tuzla's magazine *Razlika/Difference*, no. 6/7/8, 2004. With my co-translators, I translated plays by Sarah Kane, Martin Crimp, Gregory Motton, and Philis Nagy. This poem was written in relation to this experience of translating. (DD)

[73] "The rain falls in sheets" is a reference to the refrain of a famous song by the popular Croatian singer-songwriter Arsen Dedić, "Milena," which was a hit in the sixties: "Milena, Milena,/we will go out of the city/a curtain of rain falls/there's nothing here for us." ["Milena, Milena, /poćićemo izvan grada/ zavjesa od kiše pada/ nema ovdje ničega za nas"]. (DD)

some kind of liquid is constantly
pouring out.)

D: Hello, father, who is deep on this stage. On the stage with a wish in motion which is addressed as "We are the ones" "I am the one," but all that you are saying is nonsense because you must fill time, stage time, as opposed to the real, stage time/real time.

(when the girl stops crying she turns
around and sees her face in the mirror.)

D: Can you imagine, I was holding a banana in my hand, and they took it from me.

(the girl spots the boy and curiously, inquisitively
stares at him while he is peeing on the grass.)

A: Hyperbolic time is the one which devours me, digests and then defecates me. You look at me in the eyes, jealously, look at me and envy me. Hyperbolic time is the one which devours me...

D: (as if she wants to go off stage.) That site is very familiar. They were swallowing dumplings. They ate without getting filled. She was waving with her hands. She was pointing at ships that were sailing in and taking over all the space left in that story. Don't talk nonsense. I am sick of hearing how you are so full of yourself.

(the rain still doesn't stop falling. The drops
are collecting in a recess. They are a breakthrough, eat up the
hyperbolic space. Space breaks up into time. Sequences in
which The Female Writer summarizes outside sensations,
the moods of the moment, the fatal attraction of facts, the fascination
with virtual space.)

B: This was common, already, come out of that hole (she says to an invisible character on the stage.) I can't look at him (addresses The Female Writer.) LEAVE; LEAVE!

141

D: (sings) I've driven away the darkness
From this garden of fear
The synopsis is steady
The magic powder has
disappeared

B: Come on, already! Come out!
A: Stop fooling around. Who are you speaking to? Stop screaming! I can't stand screaming!

(The girl turns towards the imaginary figure which she can only see, caresses her hair, smiles and laughs.)

N: You think you're interesting? You are wrong. Everything that you're saying is dumb, empty. You are a real dumb, empty-headed Male Writer! (she turns around and leaves.)

D: Imagine that! I had to run to catch the bus, not to be late…

I had to figure out how to use the infinitive and only the infinitive. I wrote an ode to infinitives.[74] Now they give a different rhythm to the sentence. With them the rhythm in a sentence is different. Discussions about language have poisoned the environment. I don't see any way out. Who says? Why?

(Suddenly the lights go out. The stage is completely dark. The girl lights up the Spirit which sits beside her, sings an incomprehensible tune in an unfamiliar language:

Pitoti   liku   nir   jako   tuti
Tuti lipiti

DaDa.)
(everyone is crawling in the darkness, but the girl remains invisible.)

---

[74] "I wrote an ode to infinitives" refers to the battle at the time about the redefinition of the Serbian language from which the infinitive case was being eliminated as it was supposedly a feature of the Croatian language. (DD)

D: What can we do? This is awful! Every once in a while there's no power![75] All our lives those politicians have kept bullshitting. *Save power! Save power!* And now this fucking storm is saving us power!

(Curtain)

Belgrade, July 2004

---

[75] Reference to frequent power outages, restrictions when there was no power during certain times of the day during Milošević's rule. (DD)

I Hate Narration[76]

Is narration the heart of poetry
There's no poetry without a story…
stories seduce readers used to
the infinite storytelling,
Western European bourgeois discourse
stumbles over the ears of readers who recognize codes
of stories, codes of knowledge, codes of wisdom
they are for him natural, normal, normalized
reader / the critic wants what he is used to
        I HATE NARRATION
           narration tears the heart out of a poem
when the most narrative poetry with the most roundabout difficult
language speaks with its own codes, indirectly
A poem is not a closed system which reproduces itself
from one example into another, the form is the same (recognizable)
the content varies. I saw her, she moved quickly like a gazelle
her sexual being knew of all the mysteries
arcane machines that were hitting the heart of darkness, the heart of poetry
her body was diving in the dark liquid of the castle
the castle is screen white
poetry is happening between new technologies,
new realities—VR—MTV—Postcommunism
The poem breaks through reality, constructs reality
It doesn't reflect, doesn't express, doesn't tell a story
There's no universal story. All stories have been told
Poetry is a body, a passionate body   SEX SCREEN
Postsocialist reality in Serbia
is strangling the will for a poetic Eros
It's difficult to fight through the collective mud of One
Because of that the critic hates when the Other speaks with the language of
                           the first and

---

[76] Previously published in the Serbian Voivodina magazine, *TRANSkatalog*, Issue no. 5, 1996/97 from Novi Sad whose founding editor was Vladimir Kopicl. It was published in the fourth part of the book titled *Diskurzivne mašine: eseji.* In the poem, I use the reference to Robert Grenier's statement "I Hate Speech" as the proclamation "I hate narration" that refers to my negative response to the domination of narrative poetry in the Serbian culture. (DD)

inserts the language of the Other—the language of its (multiple) identities
Identities intertwine
because the Politics of the poem is the politics which moves out of control
and the JOYFUL critics JUST LIKE THE JOYFUL POLITICIANS
control the whole area OF THE POETRY THAT IS BECOMING
THE POSTCOMMUNIST OTHER
Critics with their (mis)understanding kill poetry
POETRY DOESN'T EXIST BECAUSE OF CRITICISM—to be stifled, to
                                                    be controlled
control means to have power—politicians control the space OF IDEOLOGY

The poem spreads and boldly enters the surrounding discourses. There
is no poetic discourse that is natural, recognizable
and the only correct one
which means : the heart of poetry is not narration
that sweet story which draws from Large stories which
according to Lyotard[77] fell apart, scattered, collapsed
A poem is put together from fragments of stories
It can be narrative, non-narrative and antinarrative
Jerome McGann[78] writes about that,
so do Charles Bernstein and Lyn Hejinian, as does
Marjorie Perloff
about a poem that doesn't have a predetermined form
which Americans have discussed as early as mid-twentieth century
For us there is only one acceptable form
one that is still taken for granted
That's why the majority of our poems look alike
because form, which was defined by Russian Formalists
at the beginning of the twentieth century is that which
distinguishes poetry, or prose from other discourses
which means it's not important *What* it says, it's important *How* it is said
but that basic formalism is foreign to every ideology

---

[77] Jean-François Lyotard (1924-1998) was a French philosopher, sociologist, and literary theorist. His interdisciplinary discourse spans such topics as epistemology and communication, the human body, modern art and literature and critical theory, music, film, time and memory, space, the city and landscape, the sublime and the relation between aesthetics and politics. He is best known for his articulation of postmodernism after the late 1970s.

[78] Jerome McGann (b. 1937), an American academic and textual scholar whose work focuses on the history of literature and culture from the late eighteenth century to the present.

which says poetry is that and that, it's like this and that
and everything which goes against it IS NOT poetry
But poetry is what the poet says it is
genre borders disappear, so that plays become
poetry, so that essays become poetry,
anthologies of postmodern American poetry are already
including in the general term "poetry" (not the lyric, never the LYRIC)
include the essay, play, or that which has long been known
as prose poetry or poetic prose
so the speaker of the writing moves through the varied act of writing and says
I'm exploring, I don't recognize borders, I
don't set restrictions for myself
That is why I hate Narration which is straightforward not linear
which spits on form, on the body of the text without which
it really doesn't even exist
because the body is what matters and not the thought
the text, the material, without which a single thought doesn't exist
That's why Derrida unmasked the priority of thought,
Western logocentricity[79] which is
so deeply rooted in every Western mainstream culture
including the Communist and Postcommunist countries
       It moved like the Other
Its transparent body, its organs outlined
lit up with x-rays, revived on the screen
as a dancer in the airless space
that's the poetry of the writing that's imprinted by languages
of the screen. With magnetic plates
ideology is inscribed in every incarnation
and every materialization, reification
in everyone's sexuality
because the body is that which defines us
but it too is extended, even if Postcommunist
because the dictator's will still doesn't determine the writing
of each individual who resists through writing,

---

[79] Logocentrism—is a term coined by the German philosopher Ludwig Klages in the early 1900s. It refers to the tradition of Western science and philosophy that regards words and language as a fundamental expression of an external reality. It holds the logos as epistemologically superior and that there is an original, irreducible object which the logos represents. According to logocentrism, the logos is the ideal representation of the Platonic ideal.

through ideology of textuality, meaning, the body of the text
that ideology won't allow itself to be suppressed, to be channeled, controlled
To control means to IMPOVERISH
not recognizing possibilities, not recognizing the right for extending the body
of the text
That's why in poetry, as in politics the question of control
is a question of power
ideology (what one can, what one can't, how one can, how one can't
who can, who can't, who has, who doesn't have) is a question of power
Power reproduces and shows in the image of the world that is permissible
—channeled, controlled
The poem speaks about the image of the world—is a model of the world—says
Lotman[80]—
whether we accept it as the only one which is served to us the only one that's
truthful and correct—the others then don't exist
A poem produces meaning—it's a direct product of ideology
so poems differing from the prescribed (controlled ones, meaning a priori
coded with a critic's ideology)
are not considered as poems, they show their own, alternate ideology,
they create new possibilities, for the critical establishment they are
a threat—because the world is an image they have accepted
and any other image is a threat, because it speaks of infinite
possibilities, about the exploratory spirit and the existence of the Other
And the Other has been sacrificed, the Other has been killed, the Other has
been exiled
in our heavenly Postcommunism

Poem = politics
Poem = ideology
Poem = the body of the text

In between are waves, in between are mountain ranges
in between are screens

---

[80] Juri Lotman (1922-1993) was a prominent literary scholar, semiotician, and cultural historian, who worked at the University of Tartu. He was elected a member of the British Academy, Norwegian Academy of Science and Letters, Royal Swedish Academy of Sciences and Estonian Academy of Sciences.

in between are areas between letter and letter, word and word, syntagm and
syntagm

Critical work is restrictive, it doesn't allow
anything that is occurring besides the strictly prescribed rules
It's clear what is allowed, what's possible, whose existence is validated

The pretense of lies fluttered in the wind and it stood up and thought
this world is really beautiful seen in the virtual reality of Postcommunism
a catastrophe realized in tectonic disturbances which
destroy thousands of human lives. Corpses are an everyday image
but no one gets upset anymore because the future is being realized in front of
our eyes the moment
we are watching that reality on the screen
bodies butchered, butchered minds
that beauty of disintegration, disease,
we can see that nicely in the photographs of Cindy Sherman[81]
but does reality exist that the West could read
as a code of Eastern Europe[82]

To speak of poetry, to speak of the criticism means to speak of politics, to
speak of ideology of the broadest categories of those terms
Poetry is not separate from the world or the world from poetry

I HATE NARRATION

---

[81] Cindy (Cynthia Morris) Sherman (b. 1954) is an American artist whose work consists primarily of photographic self-portraits, depicting herself in many different contexts and as various imagined characters. Her breakthrough work is often considered to be the collected "Untitled Film Stills," a series of 70 black-and-white photographs of herself evoking typical women's roles in performance media (especially arthouse films and popular B-movies). In the 1980s, she used color film and large prints, and focused more on costume, lighting and facial expression.

[82] The important question for Eastern European art after 1989 was how to interpolate Eastern European art into the history of Western art, how to construe the code which will enable reading and understanding Eastern European art. The answers are given in two books: *East Art Map: Contemporary Art and Eastern Europe*, edited by IRWIN, 2006, and *Postsocialist Condition: Politicized Art under Late Socialism*, edited by Aleš Erjavec, 2003. (DD)

Part 7: from *Ka politici nade (Nakon rata)*
(OrionArt, 2015)

"Your eyes have deposited mud"[83]

Your eyes have deposited mud
only the poem remained on the surface
made of soap suds from longing
There are no more domestic flights[84]
another war was led
secretly hidden from us
No one has informed me
that the hills are weeping
that the small branch of space
rotted in the wind
you fused a tear with the symptom
the difference has proven itself
to be fruitful
futurists have taken their seats
She walked and thought about her past lives
of female workers, suffragettes[85]
women poets
a basket full of apples tipped over
while I waited in line for heaven
You threw away the rhyme and embraced free verse
words in freedom
pattern poetry
concrete poetry movement
visual poetry

---

[83] The next six poems are from the serial work, *Diaries from the Travel (After the War),* written on a trip between Belgrade, Trieste, Duino and back to Belgrade in August 2006. I attended the "Residenze Estiva," organized by Italian poet Gabriella Musetti. They are in part one of the book, *Toward the Politics of Hope (After the War).* The phrase "Towards the Politics of Hope" refers to the work of Damir Arsenijević, Bosnian Anglicist and theoretician. The phrase "After the War" is a reference to Robert Duncan's *Ground Work—Before the War.* (DD)

[84] At the moment when the poem was written, because of the breakup of Yugoslavia there were no flights to some other parts of Serbia. (DD)

[85] Reference to a poem written by Snežana Žabić, "Na raskršću," ["At the Crossroads"] published in the anthology *Discursive Body of Poetry,* 2004, p. 41. (DD)

He forgave her everything and said
Nothing repeats itself twice
as I was standing stunned
because the film had not ended, and the film reel
was turning on empty
In the 1960s
and I don't speak Italian
in a mini skirt I'm walking down the street
dreams have disappeared
because in this poem there are no dreams
only I held on
to that metaphor
while they fought
around midnight

Please take a moment to carefully refer to the safety information card
for more information
and return it to your seats

The closest exit is a blind alley
No one expects anyone
to be there
Only a few will be able
to interpret these signs
Because she has left everything
in total disarray
An irregular diet is harmful
Damage has been sustained with the explosion
of gas on a deserted island
Everyone has abandoned it
Even the cat drank the milk
licked herself and then disappeared [86]

---

[86] This is a reference to a poem "Cat" ["Mačka"] by Natalija Marković, from her second
collection of poetry *Kiberlabaratorija* from 2007. (DD)

"That which began as an incident"

That which began as an incident
is an expected happiness[87]
     A memory comes through powerful alleys
of debauchery
     Dichotomy is in the core of a burglar
A man loses his mind, kills
the woman and leaves
     The woman falls and the scene freezes[88]
The border between the two ends, is thin
     It's completely different in his
autobiography
     He writes about growing up, maturing
and getting old, about missed opportunities
and gains
While the river overflows
the grass breaks in the hand

Before I answer
please allow me to tell you something
about transcendence and about movement and about
standing. I think that's how our culture's best
presented
His strength has been displayed
once again
He didn't allow reforms
He looked at the distant future
and realized wisdom[89]

---

[87] Reference to a 1997 Italian movie, *La Vita è Bella*, about Auschwitz with Roberto Benigni. (DD)

[88] Reference to Juliana Spahr's poems published in the book *Response* (Sun & Moon Press, 1996) from which I translated several poems. (DD)

[89] Ironic shaping of the figure of a dictator. (DD)

Smells and sounds of oriental bazaars
keep me awake and even though
I'm tired I'm not missing this superb
pleasure
Three decades, two generations, one goal
to the extent of beauty which this drama[90]
provides.

---

[90] Incorporation of the language of advertisements. (DD)

"White peaks of mountains"

White peaks of mountains
coated with silver
Low white clouds sprinkled with silver
dust
Curvy bridges
Roofs of houses
Parceled earth
my anger
my character
my boredom
my excitement
my anthem
Which one?
My own, my personal one

"I want to write"

--I want to write
--*Radi bezbednosti leta isključite mobilni telefon*
(For flight safety please keep your cellphones switched off)
--I want to write
--*Vežite pojaseve dok sedite*
(Fasten seat belts while seated)
--I want to write
--*Pojas za spašavanje je ispod vašeg sedišta*
(Life vest is under your seat)
--I stop writing

"I'll meditate on a ship"[91]

I'll meditate on a ship[92]
I won't say anything
foam, sound, *morje*[93]
I won't say anything
I'm reading Alexandra Petrova[94]
in Russian
I'm reading Maria Grazia Calandrone[95]
in Italian
Words are words, but there is no meaning
The sound and the voice, that's all that is present

I'm translating myself to you
        you to me
The coast is round almost

eyes are *очи*
beard is *борода*
mouth is *губы*
nose is *нос*
leg is *нога*
hair is *волосъи*
skirt is робка

---

[91] from *Diaries from Travels (After the War) Part One.*

[92] During one day in Trieste, Croatian poet, Marijana Šutić, living in Trieste, and Alexandra Petrova, Russian poet living in Rome, and I spent time joyfully pointing at the same words in Croatian, Serbian and Russian. (DD)

[93] *Morje*—Slovenain for "sea." (DD)

[94] Alexandra Petrova (b. 1964) is Russian poet and writer living in Rome since 1998. (DD)

[95] Maria Grazia Calderone (b. 1964) is an Italian poet, writer and playwright living in Rome. (DD)

"as if yes is"

as if yes is

si^{96}
ja^{97}

Someone has banged the door
I feel tired, I can't speak
Everything is strange
sea *morje*[98]
I speak with myself
Someone said something
I'm silent
We laugh
Everything's nice
fixed
I don't know what to say
We'll talk later
walk
speak about poetry in
Croatia, Slovenia, Serbia, Italy, Russia
I believe that everything points to something else
one thought leads to another
a cute little woman
poetessa e terrorista[99]
nuvole[100] on the sky

how to translate, so many voices
in Italy are two powerful currents
one under the influence of the Beat generation

---

[96] Si—yes in Italian.

[97] *Ja*—yes in Slovenian.

[98] *Morje*—"sea" in Slovenian.

[99] *Poetessa e terrorista*— (Ital.) woman poet and terrorist.

[100] *Nuvole*—clouds.

and another under the influence of
visual poetry, we connect those two traditions
poetry is a woman's activity
the muses have given
poets words
Poetry is the voice of a mother
an ancient voice which speaks through us
To compose sonnets
we eat afterwards, we read
talk about
Poetry dedicated to the mother
dedicated to the son
dedicated to Sylvia Plath
Allen Ginsberg and Brodsky in a poem
Discourses of pornography
Someone reads slowly
someone reads quickly
you gesticulate
Dantean poetry
Manzoni
Petrarch's line
suitcases leaning on
the pillar painted white
national languages of
monoculture
in a globalized world
Pier Paolo Pasolini
United World College of the Adriatic
Duino
Along Rilke's path
through the forest by the sea
reading Rilke in Belgrade
It's one o'clock
voices around me
it's a spectacle/ *spectacolo*
imago
I don't have a feel for languages
It's hot
I say hello

Theatre in verse
feminist poetry
sublime poetry
Russia, Russia
Where are we at halfway through the magical forest
Metrics return
I return to the inner voice
It's impossible
here and now
Laura, cicadas
I'm using a female character
She is tired, doesn't speak
But she writes
She can only write
incarnato
anche media
storie personale
e cosi[101]
my works in volumes
I love you little kitty
I kiss you on the nose
nuvole, nuvole[102]

---

[101] From Italian: "Embodied/even moderate/personal story/and so." Thanks to Vesna Obradović for her help.
[102] From Italian: "oblaci, oblaci." Thanks to Vesna Obradović for her help.

"I deal with myself"

I deal with myself
narcissism of the female writer
laughter
I anesthetize, I'm performing my poetry tonight
Good, very nice
I drank too much
I'm writing messages
Morje[103] *morje*
ciao[104]
see you soon
ciao
the phone rings
ciao
say, quickly say it
St. Petersburg, Israel, Rome
let's move on
I'll visit you in Rome some time
Come and you'll see *nuvolle*[105]
I don't want to hang out with you
she's a sister
a nurse
a nun
my sister, yours
speaking of sisterhood
half past one
when are we leaving
where are we going
with whom
Where are you, where are you
Emily Dickinson
Audre Lorde

---

[103] *Morje*—the sea in Slovenian.

[104] *Ciao*—Ital. for hi, hello, also used in Serbian.

[105] *Nuvolle*—clouds in Italian.

Hélène Cixous[106]
Rosi Braidotti[107]
What is poetry capable of
Sublime, mundane, ordinary
I love you, beg you
Freed space
Luciana, Rosanna, Maria, Maria Grazia, Gabriella
Mariana, Alexandra[108]
Morje, morje

Poetry has many languages: it may be written in a mother's tongue or in its dialects, in foreign languages, second languages, third languages...

"There exist things that a system cannot assimilate
One of them is poetry."

---

[106] Hélène Cixous (b. Oran, Algeria, 1937) is a professor, French feminist writer, poet, playwright, philosopher, literary critic and rhetorician. Cixous is best known for her article "The Laugh of the Medusa," which established her as one of the early thinkers in post-structural feminism. She founded the first center of feminist studies at a European university at the Centre Universitaire de Vincennes of the University of Paris (today's University of Paris VIII).

[107] Rosi Braidotti (b.1954) is a contemporary Italian-Australian philosopher and feminist theoretician.

[108] Italian authors: Luciana Tufani, Rosanna Crispin Da Costa, Maria Inversi, Maria Grazia Calandrone, Gabriella Musatti; Croatian author: Marijana Šutić, and Russian author: Alexandra Petrova. Thanks to Gabriella Musatti for helping to reconstruct the participants of Rezidence Estive that took part in the conversation on feminism. (DD)

Maria Grazia

Maria Grazia wants to sit at Rilke's *sto/stol*[109]
I wish the same
To be inspired by Rilke's Muse
the one who supports the face
destroys the sun
drives me crazy

> I am upset and *sedim/sjedim*[110]
> You won't *videti/vidjeti*[111] me
> *Nasmijanu/nasmejanu* [112]

The Clown's face passes before my eyes
Riječi i reči[113] come to the wall
then I pull back
because love is red like *češnja/čežnja*[114]
because love is a small Amor on your shoulders
I say, you say, we say
But there is no "we"
It's not for sure
It's not certain
It's not possible[115]

> Except in the story about someone who comes
> from the past and disappears in the past
I watch from afar and see a veil over her face
The logic of interpretation is the opposite of the principles of interpretation

---

[109] *Sto/stol* [table]—Serbian/Croatian—the author's dual identity, Croatian and Serbian, is shown in parallel usage of these languages. On a smaller scale that would be an example of translingualism.

[110] Serbian and Croatian, Bosnian, Montenegrin words for "sit."

[111] Serbian and Croatian, Bosnian, Montenegrin words for "see."

[112] Serbian and Croatian, Bosnian, Montenegrin words for "smiling."

[113] Croatian and Serbian words for "words."

[114] Poet plays with the words: Slovenian word *češnja* means *trešnja* and *trešnja* means cherry, and Serbian, Croatian, Bosnian, Montenegrin word *čežnja* means "longing."

[115] Reference to Yugoslavian nations and nationalities.

Music is a word but not the silence which is[116]
Sediments in my *langu*/tongue[117]
        (You are talking too much)
You'll interrupt silence by being quiet   or not
Listen
                        Between two formations a unique form
comes down to polarity
            Polar bears take their places

Hunters hunt fragments of narration
Poets today have a more naive relationship towards language than[118]
we used to have
The theory of poetry passes through two in-between times
in which silence is loud, bursts with sound, twitches
I live in a tiny *kut*[119] of the heart

            I don't get enthralled
            I bite
            I don't swing
            I shy away
            twisted feathers in the breeze
Silence is a threatening noise

Belgrade-Trieste-Duino-Belgrade, August 2006

---

[116] Reference to early V. Kopicl. (DD)

[117] "Language" and "tongue" in Serbian/Croatian (or in CBSM) are the same word, "jezik."

[118] The words of Andrej Medved, Slovenian poet, curator and theoretician in regard to then contemporary Slovenian poets of new generations. (DD)

[119] Croatian word for "corner."

Silence Is the Only Noise Which Threatens [120]

after Charles Bernstein

... and she orders me... come closer and knock
Because a man was created... I wish to let you know

and, he orders me, I beg you nicely
Someone has entered and slammed the door
You can write, you can pray, you can scream [121]
I want to know... those little low passions
Little by little I moved away from her anger
Someone whispered, she is immoral
She is crazy

I thought I'd collapse from shock

The smell of young wine
The smell of dew
Body odor

It has spread all over the planet

       I moved away and thought
I can't do anything about it. I can dream
dream of a bed. The bed is making faces. You can sing
You can scream. You can climb up to the sky

Created, cried, constrained,
joyful, sad, weeping

I ask myself what your name is, what you're thinking, where you're going

---

[120] From *Towards a Politics of Hope (After the War)* Part Two. The starting point of this poem is Charles Bernstein's poem "The Manufacture of Negative Experience" that I translated and published in *ProFemina*, 2003. (DD)

[121] Insisting on the usage of infinitives (see footnote 74 in play poem, "Rain"). (DD)

Then they went to the forest. Then they disappeared
at the beach. Afterwards they descended the staircase. Then
they had ice cream. Then they thought. Then they wrote
and laughed. Then they cried and ran. Then they
argued. Then later they scolded and supported wholeheartedly

I thought of you and your round eyes. Like a small
doggie. Me—around your feet. You're doing
the same

You came flustered and with a strange story. About a dark forest
and the hunters in the forest and scared wildlife. You came flustered
and said: They cried and they behaved strangely. They
lured beasts into the trap. And the horizon moved

But I had already seen all that...

The Party

I don't have the impression that something needs to be said
and I say it well
She's silent and approaches an awkward skill
I'm skilled in observation, distortion
of wisdom
We've found the blessing of chalk
in the pandemonium of hysteria
You simply couldn't tell me
You were quiet and sexy
Afterwards we went to the nearby bathtub
in which hippos/hippopotami were having a party[122]
We joined them
danced like crazy in the chaos
of the wish for the unachievable
And you didn't tell me the secret
the magic word
which initiated the sleeping passions
and the pontoon bridge swung in
the distance, but no one said
anything
At that moment I really thought something
was not right
when in the distance I heard a bull bellow
bicycles fell down
and I remained confused
Your hair danced on the water's surface,
My smile separated from my lips and
searched for your lips[123]

---

[122] The reference to Charles Bernstein's poem "The Manufacture of Negative Experience." (DD)
[123] Reference to Rosmarie Waldrop's book, *Reluctant Gravities* (New Directions, 1999), that I translated at the time. (DD)

You simply couldn't tell me,
Because we didn't understand those magic words
of the trumpet which was coming through the gothic novel

Patriots were gathering on the square and
Waving with flags
and greeting the leader
Saluting in a military standstill

We waved with our hands and passed through
By the halo of the saint whose eyes were shining
in the dark as if a cat's

Her cat came down from the screen
And comfortably seated herself in my lap[124]

Afterwards we spoke about love and hatred
About whether a female artist is only a female artist
Or is it important that she also acts in the sphere of politics

Her friends and she wanted to declare her
a politician
but we know that she is an important literary writer

You waved with your hand and said that that's all
idle gossip and that we must concentrate
on one concept and devote our whole life
to it, that in life and art
it's a question of both life and death[125]

But women have the irresistible need to
be flattered, they have an irresistible need to
be needed and they then fall in love wildly

---

[124] The reference to Natalija Marković's poem (see footnote 82). (DD)

[125] Reference to Walter de Maria's statement that circulated in Belgrade's late, analytical, conceptual art scene at the end of the 70s to mid-80s. (DD)

You said all that is idle gossip
look at a book, a screen, at a painting
at a body. That knowledge, that skill
is created through patient, tormented work

"You could say my knowledge is limited"

You could say my knowledge is limited
by gravitation. I lowered myself to the floor and began
with the exploration of mercury grains that spilled
from the thermometer.
Water in the water heater heated up to boiling.
She boiled on the road to Nowhere land.
That's where her home is and small heavenly gardens surround
the homes of the dead.[126]
She comes out to greet him, waves to him,
calls him, writes him love messages.
Gardens of poetry in her heaven are neglected,
Overgrown with weeds of narration.

Flies fly low.
Imagination releases its soul.

Near a river with lots of mosquitoes
My wish is a little twisted.
Your imagination is packed in cling wrap
Ready for sale

Apples, apples,

Roll in your conscience
And fall in weightlessness.

I really wanted to let him know
She wishes to walk with you.
I want to fly.
Do you want some tea?
Do you want a little poem?
Do you want freedom of movement
Through a weightlessness of poetry

---

[126] The reference to Rosmarie Waldrop's book, *Reluctant Gravities*. (DD)

Quickly you hide the old, yellowed manuscript.
You didn't want me to touch it.
You were afraid of an infection.
The paper was almost falling apart.
And we were breaking through a snowstorm.
Snowflakes froze on our eyelashes.
Frozen breath was barely able to separate from our mouths.
Sometimes it seemed to me that the wax petals
Were falling on top of our heads
But she knew that wasn't the truth,
That that's a dangerous delusion which takes over your mind.

A boat was sailing on the dry riverbed.
I dove my hand into sand, thinking it's water.

The desert stretched in front of your eyes,
And a hot, boiling desert sun.
In her heart she knew that that sun was the sun of love.

She knew because the tiny mice were peeking out of their hiding
places.

She walked at a firm pace towards a bright future,[127]
Like everyone else, and no one could stop them.

The river overflowed and flowed into lakes.
An airplane flew over them.
Its threatening howl spread through the valley
Inhabited by Siamese cats, small dolls, cyborgs, spiders and eagles.
The height was an issue. No one could surmount it.
Others lagged behind in the valley discouraged by despair.

---

[127] The phrase "bright future" is the ironic reference to socialist ideological discourse of a bright future. (DD)

It Is Like *Air France Magazine*[128]

between Copenhagen and…* *thank you very much*[129] *
he jokes * very funny *
we're going to have some fun * you put lipstick on your lips * while I wait
for the plane to take off * in the end * in exile * poetry
and (male) gender * I am overjoyed * I'm very happy *
little girls walk the deserted beach * jargon * dominates
French * underwater * in a cave * in the womb * the land of
the Mayas * utopia * atopia * when I close my eyes * I see
your face * don't speak nonsense because I won't listen *
she's very funny and relaxed * when she jokes * when
she laughs * *we like it* * compensation * I loved it *
simulation * they run to hide and to light a cigarette * *škure*[130] *
light falls on the face of justice * we will
never reach * fuss * I am drinking juice * it's more natural than
the natural * I am eating a croissant * real French *
from the airport * you're reading about French theoreticians * but
you cannot live off of theory * sneakers * you will be
one of the greatest * air fans * heaters * horticulture *
more natural than the natural * more original than the original *
more authentic than the authentic
–FAKES–who are you fooling * I am a cuttlefish * I am an octopus *
a botanist cares about the garden * more authentic than the authentic * kitsch
* a man in an expensive suit with a tie * flies * *belle*
devant le prototype * jaguar mutates * a woman with a bomb *
she doesn't speak but acts * *agency* * a female terrorist is looking at her
watch waiting for a signal[131] * puts on make-up * underneath * Narciso
Rodriguez *parfum for her* * pink shoes with high
heels * pulp fiction * *technologie* **hybride**

---

[128] From *It Is Like* Air France Magazine *(after the war) Part Three*. This magazine was used as source material for this and the next poem. This and the next poem refer to the British playwright, Martin Crimp, and his play, *Attempts on Her Life* that I translated with Vanda Perović for the magazine *Razlika/Différance* from Tuzla, Bosnia and Herzegovina, thanks to the invitation of Nedžad Ibrahimović, Editor-in-Chief of the magazine. (DD)

[129] Originally in English, French or Italian if in italics.

[130] *Škure*—Croatian-Dalmatian for shutters.

[131] Reference to Ivana Sajko, Croatian playwright's play *Woman Bomb*. (DD)

Haute Performance * performs her dance in a new
metallic car * I'll never be lonely *
I'll never be hurt * I'll never be
abandoned * because speed is perfection * because luxury is
normality * because * *5 dollars to catch the bell* * that's
the real price for all extravagance * *she* * *che bella* *
bella * *bella idea*[132] * you need protection * you need
change * you need innovation * vuarnet
sunglasses * *la legend* * in a perfectly designed
room with a purple two-seater sofa * purple table * purple chair *
purple and white walls * in which the newest model of a black elegant
Samsung screen dominates * Karin Rechid
explains it to you * Cairo * Prado, MOMA New York,
Canada * you'll realize that only destruction makes sense *
obsessed with terrorism * Paris, oh Paris * new
magic formula in Montreal and Munich * New Eve
in a romantic dress will take a bite of Nina Ricci's new apple *
the new magical fragrance * and he will know what
that formula *gentleman farmer "be & behave"* means *
no matter what you choose to be * hedonist, DJ, yuppie * think of the speed
that frees you * think of security * about that
which is reasonable and brings excitement * dynamic design
* a mix of glamor and latent energy * frees the mind *
encourages the imagination * be creative * be yourself *
be innovative * choose heaven on earth * a bottle
of the perfume cosmophobia * buy this wristwatch and you will receive more
than a watch

---

[132] Reference to Italian poetry ensemble, Rapsodi Gruppo Fonographico, who gave a performance at Residenze Estive. (DD)

"We are separated by continents…"

We are separated by continents * they sit beside
me and are speaking in some Nordic language * The story develops
around the visit to the Taj Mahal * we see him in
the photographs with family, besides his car,
in his office, in front of his villa * a successful
man smiles

At the age of 44, he greets us while he sits behind
the semicircular desk with a glittering screen
        A long time ago there was a woman whose
childhood resembled Hugo's *Les Miserables*, but whose
later life had an aura of a Proust's ball

You cannot resist the beauty of Louisiana * The city with lots
of bicycles * at 36 she became a famous designer *
that a comfortable way of living has made meaningless *
at 36 she left her family and became a terrorist * which
has made her life meaningful * A pedestrian street in the center
of the city * Norm/normality * exclusive * patriotic *
treasonous * vomited * unfathomable * witty *
charming * irresistible * charm * joke * prank *
very very witty * funny * pointless-
meaningful * we all understand, but what does it mean,
how can we make use of it practically * in exile *
in isolation * he is rational to the core * he has no
imagination * I don't have any either * I don't have a sense for
humor * I don't laugh * I'm dead serious * comfortable
small talk relaxes * we are very social * humor
socializes

But the city of lights is also the city of darkness * come, spend
a nice evening with us, even though we don't know you,
we will offer you any consolation, protection
                              because the protagonists of this
                      dance
are dancing the dance of life and death

Invest in the future * come to Madagascar *
a dramatic environment will return you to nature * bays,
lagoons, volcanic eruptions of your emotions will wake up in
you the primordial savage

While she flies in the wild blue space, she is daydreaming about
the vast freedom of blue space, her
smile is inviting you to rise into an adventure from which
there is no return * wilderness, freedom
                    discover freedom in and out of yourselves

May 2nd, New York[133]

Sarah Morris (1967)
painter and film director, great paintings refer
to the paintings created in the early part of the 20th century, *hard edge*
geometric
abstractions and invoke a history of a modernist network.
She's not in formalism. Her compositions indicate
the network of power and the system of communication encoded in
the architecture of late capitalism.
                    She's interested in Las Vegas hotels and how
they integrate gigantic electronic billboards which
don't advertise products but themselves, echoing
airtight self-referential nature of the large portion of
abstract painting. She imitates how architecture
serves as a seductive sign of corporate power—in
this case the power of industrial entertainment…

---

[133] The poem was written during a walk-through of New York streets or at museums. Parts that deal with artists Sarah Morris, Jeff Wall or Piet Mondrian's *Broadway Boogie Woogie* were written by the technique of appropriation: I translated the museum's plaques of their works. (DD)

While You Read, I Sleep
(After the War)

I

I don't want water more than I want sand[134]
everyone is running while I stand
I don't want a duck more than I want a building
a corporate power of capitalism
—left and right—
I've invented attention so that I could grab (stomp on) a bush
of conscience
in the Chinese quarter–*skyscrapers* and a duck quietly descend
I don't want flowers just like I don't want jello
only the confused can say—Beijing in full view
no one remembered anyone—green blue
purple and white—textuality
9/11
I don't want more words from
the peaks of pine trees—disco stage
and the fascination with contemporary art. On Times Square
New York Times
I don't want anything that doesn't
belong to me—when you say I
you think she—while cameras are clicking—when I say I
I am thinking of you—I am thinking
how nothing remains behind
as long as the skirt is wrinkled
I don't want to say I don't want
I am going around in circles—it's a dangerous
time—you don't want to say I don't
want—that's why you slow down—
that's why we're going around in circles
tourists are feeling well
as are search dogs—everyone

---

[134] This poem has many references to Charles Bernstein's poems. (DD)

is running only I'm walking
and I keep stopping then I write

II

what motivates you when you sleep—models of
transcendency—brutality everywhere—
a kind of senseless boredom—buildings are bleak
as we speak at Columbia University—I enter
a bookstore and see myself across in the room where the conference
was taking place—the view out of the window unveils window washers on
the nearby building

the school bus and a police car
dogs in the street, stop and lead
on to Broadway when I think of the key word I don't understand in a
sentence
uiki—is alienation what is in the question, the epoch of digitalization
closed, forgotten space—large dimension photos
organic forms and networks of abstraction—forgotten
spaces are clearly without a sense of smell or taste
while petals ruthlessly fall
from trees like confetti at a poets'
party—Arakawa[135] and Madeline Gins[136]—painted
Abigail Child[137]
Essentially I am safe
I won't turn around
or speak
because rhyme slows the rhythm of the city
the net/grid/—we need a good story
nothing good comes out from being able to pick where to

---

[135] Arakawa (1936-2010) was one of the founding members of Japaneese avant-garde collective
Neodadaism. From 1961, he lived in New York and worked with his partner and wife, Madeline
Gins.
[136] Madeline Helen Gins (1941-2014) was an American artist, architect and poet who worked
with her partner and husband, Arakawa.
[137] Abigail Child (b. 1948) is an American filmmaker, poet and writer, active in experimental
writing and media since the 1970s.

go while
hunger remains for simulation
stimulated steam
stream

III

becoming silenced means to uncover the horror of speech—
the power of the media
ethics of behavior—light effects on the surface of water
and on the surface of a canvas and on an ad and digital
photo—on
a celluloid tape—discarded steel—rusted river—
bagels with
cream cheese—hypnosis of spring—perpetuated
observations
journalists run up to the 12th floor—we sit on newspapers
It's nice to settle in overcrowded corners
of financial impotence—
of traumatized surfaces of polyvalent signs—
female artists worry
about the surface of the canvas just as male poets worry about
financial turnovers
because there is too much money there and very little careful observation
because everything remains
on the surface of the fabric and in the shine of the mirror weakness is
impossible
to say
who will go into which direction if we're not more tolerant
We will accept
a tortilla and jump into the water of the side salad
I'm a little archaic because outside there's thunder but not raining
Only the yellow nickel-plated coin falls to the ground, on the asphalt
because it didn't know in which direction to turn

IV

my word came toward yours and they went together on a trip
she's happy because there is no substitute because

restrictions vanish and while I accept old currency to
rake it all up
which was only mentioned at that moment when in thought
she backed away
in front of the enormity of flight just like a river pauses
when a hand touches a bend
because the circle doesn't close in the gilded base of light-colored
ads of memory

*

Jeff Wall

With his presence he renews the pictorial heritage with
fictional film techniques. From 1991, some of his
images were created digitally

V

while the butterfly landed above the valley of production I didn't
want to
look back at the apocalyptic abstraction before
media pictures
filled all my imagination
and when the personal drama becomes common
and when it becomes the dust of the smiles of all that are present in the
auditorium
texts will dance in new contexts
and we will be on a safe slippery terrain
of hybrid chromosomes and heroes

Broadway Boogie Woogie
and the mythic frames of modernism

—make sure you come
—it's time for us to change the world
—unpleasantness
—guilt
—misfit

We are confronted with the same problems
so in order not to have to think of that
I went in another direction
You have to show a different model
She left everything subordinate to her passion for writing
As an inventor many doors
were opened to him
The connection between colors, the movement and the function of machines
remained unclear
From the east to the west, from the west go towards the east
That and that avenue, that and that street, that and that number

the rule of emptiness
(after the war)[138]

we want to develop something * but we don't know what * we want to reach
something * but we don't know what * we want to be somewhere * but we
don't know where * the concept of space leads to a reduction in tension *
let's be more tolerant * the concept of the mind brings us to magnolias in the
garden of vertigo * that is how the rule of the background is created in such a
way * in the sky-blue color of a baroque building * kinetics of bends *
mysticism and poetry * the cold of coat * blister's bee * let's be more
tolerant * your intolerance is threatening to me * flamboyant threat of a bite
* bring a feminist * but make sure she is pretty[139] * i don't want to say
anything* about the process of writing * about the production of illusions *
allusion leaps onto a lollypop * cats get attached to those who take care of
them in a strange way * that's love * long ago in 2010 i didn't know all that
could happen * wars were behind us * hunger and other new illnesses were
raising havoc * i began to do new research so i could find a vaccine that
would keep me awake * but a transgender person came up to me and asked
me when i had become a woman * i was surprised by such a question
because darkness was brutally descending onto the deserted fields of the
empty screen which froze the picture long ago in the year 2010 and the
citizens of that ghost town didn't know what to do with themselves and
whether a new disease was approaching or a new war which would destroy
the rest of the cells of their organisms * everyone believed it had to do with a
wide ranging conspiracy aimed at disabling us from leading normal lives *
feminists know how to be strenuous and exclusive * locked in a closet they
lose a connection with reality * we wanted to resist politics * the painter sat
by the canvas and painted ethereal beings in the shape of young women *
they are the losers * they don't have jobs * they are afraid so don't dare to
confront the harsh circumstances that shackled them * typical new york food
* combinatorics i don't understand * while i go around town you ask me
what are my political views * you know i am anxious because negative
answers are unacceptable * because on the dock there are a bunch of
hydrangeas so i ask myself how i belong there with my story * that year it

---

[138] The poem was written while thinking about the siege of Sarajevo. (DD)

[139] It is said that during the demonstrations against Milošević, the democratic leader, Zoran
Djindjić, said this. (DD)

was winter when hunger and harsh life conditions had left their mark * we
buried the corpses in the backyard in the once beautiful gardens * star wars
has done its job * people couldn't stand it anymore * they'd fall into a coma
or they would be overcome with insurmountable anger * they would destroy
everything in front of them * i was afraid to leave home barely even to fetch
water * we drank rainwater * and we all knew that it was a matter of a
conspiracy which would lead to barbarous liquidations * i looked at old
books written in an incomprehensible language that few people knew * the
stench of corpses spread everywhere * no one remained untouched * i was
obsessed with photographing it * i wanted to leave the mark from this
draconian time * but i was afraid to leave the house * infections were
spreading * at first people would get sick mentally * they would stop
behaving like human beings * they became dogs cats or plants * then their
bodies would suddenly begin to deteriorate * i was afraid for myself and my
loved ones * we were still able to cope with the hope that we would survive *
only sometimes i would fall losing hope * which was dangerous considering
i wasn't sure i would be able to return from that state * phones were not
working and any means of communication was lacking * all until at some
moment we developed our ability to communicate through telepathy * soon
we began to believe in the occult * in everything we were able to discard in
the past heartlessly * i didn't know where to hide so as not to be exposed
more than necessary * i would put my head in the sand or i would read
graphic novels which had once been so popular * people tried to overcome
alienation * we slept next to each other in order to warm up * in order to feel
the warmth of another human being * it was a feeling we had forgotten * we
learned how to talk all over again to walk again as if doing this for the very
first time * we could not sleep at night * the air was filled with different
sounds * human voices * the noise of machines and cars * but without
physical proof they had really surrounded us * i was afraid to leave my
hallway * the world seemed dangerous * destroyed * broken * and in that
environment ourselves were breaking and every attempt to try to restore them
was once more prevented * stores had not been open a long time or people
were bypassing them because they believed that an overabundance of goods
in them would create a particular dependence which was unhealthy and
would lead to the strangest damage both psychological and physical and they
were sure that such a materialistic civilization would lead to ruin * i was not
sure what to do with myself * i walked the same path to the bed to the
bathroom to the room to the kitchen * it was a simulation of ancient rituals
we had long abandoned * as humans we discarded it and now in misery all

that remained was to devise new trite rituals so as to be able to reconnect with energies which had given us meaning and restored the very vitality to exist on this planet * i forgot how to write and how to talk * i still moved in some half-conscious state of being * some new animal species had emerged that we knew nothing about some new plants * we feared we would have to start all over again * who are we now * everyone asked the same question * spatial and time dimensions gained new meaning and new forms and we knew the time had come for the uncertain restoration lies ahead[140]

---

[140] Published in the Special Serbian issue of *Atlanta Review* SP 2021 in a slightly different form.

Odsevi (Reflections)

Ave gratia plena[141]

Reflections, corso, Bazelj, H&M, Zara, thunder, noise,
odsevi (reflections), a little boat, ooo linden in *lipnju*,[142] a weeping willow,
flowers, coast, Ljubljanica,[143] Hey I need to tell you something,
mama, mama, mama, mommy, are you on a diet, yes
and on a rigorous one, no chance, *znaš kaj me zanima*,[144] in
Pyramid,[145] order right away, *kaj, a res*,[146] O.K. sure, ha
ha, ha

On pride,[147] *odsevi* (reflections), *za polpon užitek*,[148] Fabiani,
Little goldfish, *nazaj, nazaj*,[149] *Ribji trg, Sadjarsko vrtluarsko
društvo*,[150] *kako se vratijo*,[151] *ogledi mesta s ladjić*,[152]
since 1957, Darila,[153] Rokus,[154] Rifts, Prešern,[155] WC,
Strikarjeva street, Cankarjevo *nadbrežje*,[156] allowed for

---

[141] From the Catholic church in downtown Ljubljana, L. for "full of grace," first uttered by Archangel Gabriel in Annunciation. (DD)

[142] in Croatian, "lipanj," "June."

[143] River that flows through Ljubljana.

[144] In Slovenian, "Do you know what I am interested in?"

[145] A pizzeria in Ljubljana.

[146] In Slovenian, "Kaj" – "What," "res" – "true."

[147] In Slovenian, "He comes."

[148] In Slovenian, "For a complete pleasure."

[149] In Slovenian, "back"

[150] In Slovenian, "Fruit and Gardening Society."

[151] In Slovenian, "How they returned."

[152] In Slovenian, "Sightseeing Tours by Boat."

[153] In Slovenian, "Giftshop."

[154] In Slovenian, "Press House Rokus."

[155] The most important Slovenian Romantic Poet, France Prešern (1880-1849).

[156] Nadbrežje—embankment, thanks to Alenka Jovanovski, Slovenian poet and translator. (DD)

kolesarje,[157] Pharmacy, Centralna lekarna, Prešernov square,
cin-cin, Kavarna,[158] Zlatarna Celje,[159] Centropmerkur, Ura,[160]

12. 6. Koper

Sometimes I would stand on a corner to see the light * hiding
from it * that is the corner in which there is a shadow when
I am not bewitched by the war * I am watching how the rest of the world
rots * on the screen * *deklica je sedla za mizo*[161] and ate
* that's how I speak Slovenian * we sit and our heads ache *
stomach * we yearn for a sip of salted water * submarine *
navigational systems * I am falling into a horror of insecurities *
what would another woman do * *globoko*[162] inside you *
global *identiteta*[163] * hybrid subject *

Ljubljana, June 8th, 2007

---

[157] Allowed for cyclists, thanks to Alenka Jovanovski for the clarification.

[158] In Slovenian, "a coffee house."

[159] In Slovenian, "a jewelry store chain, Celje" (Celje is a town in Slovenia).

[160] In Slovenian, "watch."

[161] In Slovenian, "Girl sat down at the table."

[162] In Slovenian, "deep inside you."

[163] In Slovenian, "identity."

A Non-Narrative Poem of Poetry[164]

after Vlada Martek, Michael Palmer, Slobodan
Tišma, Vladimir Kopicl and Rosmarie Waldrop

       She is the one who hinted at this
empty space disappeared beyond reach
       The one who vacated this space
was   empty   empty   empty
       the space is reoriented, institutions occupy
minds, the invasion on my integrity

       Little Dubravka, extend your hand to the palm, here's my hand's
                                          palm
A butterfly that closes its wings, spreads its mind
       Little Dubravka, flies fly, people have
ill intentions

       You returned to poetry, in despair,
helpless to move

       Hills are created in the mountains
blue-white sky, color spreads

Don't be afraid in the darkness of the sea
They extend their hands and show me their palms
in desperation, you cannot even cry

       There were wars in the dark
the machine which produces small leaves,
pages of books

       A book opens
       A book closes

---

[164] The title comes from Gertrude Stein's "Winning His Way. A Narrative Poem of Poetry," published in translation in *ProFemina* in 1996. (DD)

In the darkness, I'm afraid
that the moment will not come
when the rosary will approach me,
show me the palm of the hand in dark blue
despair, desperation

      It's dark and very sad
everything that has happened

      The book opens
      The book closes
      The book is writing itself

I'm not sane when I say, "I'm overcome by heat."

      Small pandas fall which will never
give up and will never understand
how cruel the world is in which they've found themselves

      Pay attention to how many black veils
have come down from the sky, but everything still ended
quickly, even though infinity gaped over the abyss

Someone would have been my substitute, would have taken care of me

      Waves that I *sjećam*[165]
are caught in the attention net of memory
      The construction of memory

      It's unforgettable to sit at the beach and *smijati se*[166]
      The eyes are teary, the head falls on the pillow
on a shoulder
      A poem writes itself in the rhythm of movement

---

[165] Croatian, "sjećam" for "remember."
[166] Croatian, "smijati se" for "laugh."

Dear Darija,[167] when you don't write to me, I
Worry. What would Alexmontenegro[168] say
A monk is upset because we came
doesn't wish to explain anything[169]
Through a crack in the wall a fly barely
flees through and I leave as I have come

but a much more complicated
world is left behind

He is worried,
I am nervous

The poem doesn't wish to write itself when I want it to
The poem writes itself when I close my eyes
The poem writes itself when the book

closes/opens

Don't tell me about that
how the heart is beating when the book

closes/the heart opens

Palm, palm, open your palm for me
Pred-pjesnik[170] is a romantic with a flaw

a safe *mjesto,*[171] mythical place in an empty
space of paper, paper universe
takes me under its control

---

[167] Croatian poet and critic Darija Žilić. (DD)

[168] Montenegrin scholar of American studies, Aleksandra Nikčević Batričević. (DD)

[169] The reference is a negative response to the Orthodox Serbian monk at an Orthodox monastery in the city of Cetinje, Montenegro, during the visit by international conference members organized by the Department of English and American Studies from the Faculty of Nikšić, when the monk understood that our hosts were of Montenegrin identity—which points to the disputes between Montenegrin and Serbian Orthodox churches in Montenegro. (DD)

[170] The term *pred-pjesnik* (pre-poet) was introduced by the Croatian artist and poet, Vlado Martek. See https://jacket2.org/commentary/elementary-processes-poetry-redefining-field-vladomartek-croatian-conceptual-poetry-1970. (DD)

[171] Croatian for "place."

I'll let you know how I can't move
A dance isn't the same as standing on a sandy beach
The place I walk on
on which I meet/don't meet
myself

The same moment I think
How difficult it is to stand out
from the surface

I'm very sad and angry
I cannot move from my spot
There in a small cove of your shoulder I hide

If the book has opened
If the book wrote itself

I haven't moved
(*you can't deal with yourself*)
I haven't shifted

Who is *the Other* in this story

Don't be angry

If the cyprus tree is perched
I'm sad
If the palm has shown the path
the butterfly has moved into the darkness
Don't be angry
Nataša, *gdje si*? [172]

English words come out of nowhere
and I'm falling through numbers into hopelessness

---

[172] Montenegrin, feminist activist, playwright and prose writer, Nataša Nelević, studied General
Literature with me. "Gdje si" is Croatian, Bosnian and Montenegrin for "Where are you?" (DD)

Lancuni i plahte [173]

Some chores must be completed
as you are writing, you release yourself from sadness
Šalica[174] is on the table, illogicality

under the table

While passivity walks, weight gravitates

If the tide reaches out, you'll feel insecure
If the flame generates water, I'll be safe
If a story becomes mourning, it won't return
If an absurdity goes through the letter, it cries itself out
If a machine picks a place, muteness will return

I bear a grudge on myself, because the true
path is not improving

Because I've come too early, I won't be able to wait for myself
too late
If I've come too late
I won't be able to wait for my voice

And so the *pjesma*[175] writes itself, in spite of the rage and sadness
But, it won't wait for me because I'm always late
Unable to move, *točka*[176] that doesn't move
In relation to the horizon
up and down
A point[177] that doesn't move
in relation to the dramaturgy of *svijeta*[178]
Has moved a little

---

[173] *Lancuni* Dalmatian Croatian, *plahte* Croatian for "sheets," "i" is "and."

[174] Croatian for "tea/coffee cup."

[175] Croatian for "poem."

[176] Croatian for "dot/period."

[177] Reference to T. S. Eliot' line "At the still point of the turning world" from First Quartets, "Burnt Norton," from *Four Quartets*.

[178] Croatian for "world."

189

Lijevo[179] and right
up and down

The poem is writing itself, because the poem isn't speech
A poem doesn't need to be written because it
in itself already exists
A *pjesma*[180] which says yes, opens to the world
The *pjesma*   which says yes, follows its movement
along the piece of paper, the wall of a gallery

And that's how a poem is not written, because
it won't agree to become material

The poem releases my anger

If poetry again matters today,
why and how
How is it written it asks about what
I mean, how and why
and to whom do I matter

Suppress anger, rage towards oneself

Someone who is laughing is not satisfied with themself
Netko tko se smije[181] leads the poem on a leash
the leash of wishes
the leash of happiness

If I measure happiness with sadness, I'm not here
If my glass says hello, a prayer falls
into the water

In the hopelessness of sadness I am *bijesna*[182] with myself

---

[179] Croatian for "left."

[180] Croatian for "poem."

[181] Croatian for "someone who is laughing."

[182] Croatian for "upset, furious, enraged."

If the self cannot be expressed the poem

                              will leave me behind

And I won't let it

If the sky is blue, the abyss is black
If the suitcase is a cookie, I'm the handle
If the abyss falls, I fall after it

        Self-hatred is not the answer, because
there is no answer, which is comforting
        I don't want to be comforted because the chain of wishes
                            has been initiated
Happiness is not in the heart, if the heart is not in the right place, *mjesto*[183]
moves
        If the heart jumps, the *pjesma* writes itself
by itself it has extended the hand to mark
                      the territory
        If the poem has written itself, it has not
                  made easier the impossibility
                      of movement
I have not moved because the circle has been closed
The bag is open
If the poem keeps quiet, I yell
                frantically scream
It screams at me, I retreat
If the poem is writing itself, it writes itself
because if it's that significant *riječ*[184] which
pulls the energy of the line after itself
takes back to the energy of the line
lineation won't flood me
                I retreat, fall through
If the poem enters a dialogue with *pjesma*[185]
                I want to retreat
                I retreat and scream at myself

---

[183] Croatian for "place."

[184] Croatian for "word."

[185] Croatian for "poem."

A poem never gives up
Nothing falls through which isn't maintained
        I wish to survive on the surface
Who said that the poem yearns
Who said that *pjesma* wants
            to *utjeloviti*[186]

       There's no excuse for your
        disturbed state, for your stupidity, Poem
         Little Dubravka has hidden, because
she cannot stand the burden of the poem and
its energy and its despair

If it says that she must move
it stands
          in infantility of infinitives
and they're infinite, never
          ending like *pjesma*[187]

If a poem is an open book,
      a letter works on its behalf
because rage is in the core of stupidity

         You are a very beautiful Madam Poem
         You are very smart/dumb
Think of yourself, because whoever worries
about *pjesmi*, will ask what is important there

Except to say
      that the poem begins
          and ends
      And someone has to take care of oneself
And the one who doesn't know how to take care of a poem
               needs to learn how
      because if the person says that they don't know
who will

---

[186] Croatian for "embody."

[187] Croatian for "poem."

believe them
It's impossible for the poem to say no
if it always says yes/no

If I'm writing, you are typing
If I'm standing, the poem walks

Pjesmo! Pjesmo, where are you going?
If I don't want to ask, I won't know
I cannot
If I want to change, the poem is here
I'll direct all my anger at you
Poem

Why won't you allow me to love you
Pjesmo I don't love you, because poetry
is insufficient

If *pjesma* is sufficient, I'm not
Don't be upset, *Pjesmo,* with me
because I'm helpless

If helplessness enters a poem, I am unable to move
If you haven't slept, *Pjesmo*, I can't help you

If you're fighting with your ego you are not in *pjesmi*

You're very stupid, Poem, while I'm smart

But the anger that you foster will not
help you to change the range of stupidity
When you speak, then you are quiet or *šutiš*[188]
I don't want to hurt you, *Pjesmo*
I will hurt myself

If a poem is constantly changing, I *šutim*
No one will know the depth of stupidity, Poem

---

[188] Croatian for "keep quiet."

If you're sad I'll comfort you

If you want to cry, *Pjesmo*
         The poem will comfort you
Who has fallen out of favor
              will fall even lower
It's not the poem who is begging
I am begging it

Please, *Pjesmo,* support me in this
Be merciful
If stupidity is limitless, I'm limited
Don't waste time while you wait, I am waiting
Hunger of the poem is not the hunger for stupidity, and it is here
Even if I'm not, I am not, and if I am I am
I won't go anywhere without you

I got married to stupidity
There stupidity is magically magnificent

The poem which doesn't think of itself is not *pjesma*, it's sadness
Pjesmo, think of yourself in order to avoid stupidity
If stupidity is the sea of possibilities, deny yourself
On the planet of stupidity small poems dream
Pjesmo, if you miss, let the abyss crush you
Those who speak, are carefully *šute*[189]
Never leave me, *Pjesmo*
If I stand, I walk, the tongue says stupid things
Every moment stupidity plunders, *Pjesmo*
If stupidity doesn't abandon me, *Pjesma* will
Pjesmo, pjesmo, I'll read you your rights, so
                    you won't do more stupid things
Stupid *pjesma* is in the power of reason, I am not
If I confront stupidity, I'll confront
             you *Pjesmo*
If you widen my horizons, close the window to
                   Pjesmi

---

[189] Croatian for "silent, quiet."

There isn't that poem which would cancel

                                    sadness of stupidity

If stupidity spawns in a poem, I'll

                                    leave it

Poem, *Pjesmo* enlighten me

If you enlighten me with stupidity, Poem

                        I'll die again

On the way to a poem I need to take a rest

If *pjesma* charms me, stupidity abandons me

If the poem abandons me, stupidity increases

Pjesmo, Pjesmo don't be stupid. I'm dying again

If I shake hands with stupidity, *pjesma* abandons me

Don't abandon me, *Pjesmo*, sadness increases

If sadness is stupidity, *pjesma* stumbles

                           and I'm defending myself

               I'll perish from stupidity

               Don't cry dear Poem,

I'm crying, you are laughing

            you're laughing at me, dear *Pjesmo*

If I wish to enter *pjesmu*, I want to become a poem

You're crying dear Poem, and I'm laughing

                        I'm *smijem* at you

If the sky has denied *pjesmu*, I'm recreating it out of

                          ashes

Dear *Pjesmo*,[190] don't end up in a book

        be a burning bush in the sea of love

While I search for your meaning

               I'm creating it from ashes

If the Phoenix is a bird, ashes begin to speak

                     through a Poem

because *pjesma* has hidden itself in a book which

---

[190] CBSM languages have seven cases and depending on the use of the word, the ending of the word changes, so you have *pjesma, pjesmu, pjesmi*, etc., but it's the same word—poem.

burns in the holy bush
Protect me *Pjesmo*
       When I discard the poem, it returns
When it returns it's gone

Dear *Pjesmo* do you yearn for a book
       if a book is a bush of love that is ablaze

I love you *Pjesmo*, don't abandon me
       If I move towards you, extend your hand
             I'll go around you

If I change, *pjesma* sees through me
       Poem recognizes me and will not leave me
If I move forward, *pjesma* returns me to itself
If I return to myself, I return to it
       In the book in the book is *Pjesma*
       which yearns for extratextuality
If I yearn for a poem, I yearn for you
       because words in a chain of happiness
             move away

While I think that it's in my hand
it disappears from the view, as it becomes non-material
       If matter is the mother of a poem
the view falls on the page that has written itself

       Self-awareness of *pjesme* is searching for a space for itself
       It's not certain it can handle the emptiness
             of the surface

Dear Poem, the agony quickly disappears
and I have reconciled with the sea
       It leaves me because I want an empty page

       The tarmac remains behind us like the sea
into the altitude of the empty page

in the landscape of the sky *krajolik*[191]

     Poem don't leave me

If language has separated from language[192]

     I'll fly off the paper tarmac

                             into a cry

     Dear Poem, don't cry

mountains and the tarmacs have mixed with one another

while the plane takes off into the white cloud of

bjeline[193] of paper

     Pjesmo, I love you passionately, don't

leave me

     If I cry I am crying for you,

because I don't see how I can keep you

     If I part from you, it'll be such a great misfortune

     If the page betrays me, I'll betray the poem

and if it leaves me

     Obje[194] are sad and are crying

     I don't want sadness, I want happiness

If the *pjesma* has relieved pain, I'm

              happy, because I'm sad

because pain and sadness have overpowered *pjesmu* and

it disappears in the haze

     If the *pjesma* leaves me, it has left

                itself

And I become uncertain

     That's why I dared *in šutnji*[195]

     The empty space is not the same as is

a piece of paper in a *pjesmi*

     That is why both the poem and I are sad

     If the chain of events starts

pjesma will fall into the fire

---

[191] *Krajolik* in Croatian is "landscape."

[192] Out of Serbo-Croatian now we have Croatian, Bosnian, Serbian and Montenegrin (CBSM).

[193] Croatian for "whiteness."

[194] Croatian for "both of us."

[195] Croatian for "in silence."

      If it leaves me, I'll cry because
sadness is infinite
      If I lose you, *Pjesmo,* I lose myself
in you and tears won't touch the foundation of sadness
because only the *pjesma* knows there's no exit
      When a tear touches a cloud, the river dries up
I'm not ready for that kind of expression, because it
leaves the poem building it up

Podgorica airport, October 2010

Note: When I'm overcome with despair, I think I'll write a poem. Can a feeling of stupidity be softened by a poem? I don't know. I began with the early poetry of Slobodan Tišma[196] and Vladimir Kopicl,[197] keeping in mind the conceptual tendency in contemporary American poetry. Self-referentiality and self-awareness in poetry were a large part of my writing process from the end of the sixties til the beginning of the eighties. And then I was besieged by the short, absurd language games of Vlado Martek.[198] Again, self-referentiality and pseudosententiousness are in question, which show in the absurd pseudo-poetic, pre-poetic expression in (the post-poetic) postgenre. These poems master and confront sadness and pain. (Martek and Mladen Stilinović[199]). The poem closes in its self-referential world at a potent moment—a time when poetry again matters on the Internet, a time of global crisis, and a moment in the Serbian poetic culture when there was a yearning and madness for American poetry, especially in the new generation of poets.

---

[196] Slobodan Tišma, Serbian poet, conceptual artist, rock musician and prose writer, see: https://jacket2.org/commentary/slobodan-tisma

[197] Vladimir Kopicl, Serbian poet, conceptual artist, anthologist, translator of American poetry and recently prose writer.

[198] Vlado Martek, see note 170.

[199] Mladen Stilinović (1947-2016) was an internationally recognized Croatian conceptual artist.

Part 8: New Poems

A Fairy Tale Poem about a Keyboard[200]

in a sitting/*sjedećem* or lying position eyes slide
over the screen/*zaslonu*[201] while the fingers jump and tap
on the keys/*tipkama* of the keyboard/*tipkovnice* and the foam/*pjena* of
foamy/*pjenušavog* champagne or foamy
poetry/*pjesništva* spills out of a glass and falls on the floor while my drunken
fingers stagger and my head is totally
in the clouds—which is after all appropriate
for a female poet—HERE / *OVDJE* I REFER TO THE FACT THAT POETRY IS
ALWAYS / *UVIJEK* GENDERED

> —i dreamt of my dead mother and of how a caterpillar slithers on
> my rotten silk which is falling out of an old armoire and with an
> ornament it frames every twitch of the head or the belt which
> springs behind my grandmother's lacy old shirt/WE DON'T SAY
> GRANDMA WE SAY NONA—says Tamara to her daughter—we say
> nona[202]—nona is an old lady—and my head is in vertigo within the
> circle of its own magic and the magic of the keyboard/*tipkovnice*
> and the magic of champagne and the magic of poetry while little
> girls/*djevojčice* are running through a girl's room as an important
> place/*mjestu* of gender socialization—they will always/*uvijek* find
> themselves in a theatrical situation of mutual
> confession/*ispovijedanja* of a girl/*djevojčica* to a girl/*djevojčici*

—i dreamt that my keyboard/*tipkovnica* is crashing on the cliffs of certain
unstable balance in which your language finds a shelter because language is
like a sea full of corals and shells and jellyfish but also plastic **POLLUTION**
which pollutes the environment/*okolje* in which we are soaked in order to
get more and more wealth

---

[200] In this and the next poem, I worked with different kinds of fonts. (DD)

[201] Here I use Serbian and Croatian words next to each other. (DD)

[202] Tamara Polić, a friend from Rijeka, from my teenage days. When I met her after twenty years, she told me how the newcomers to Rijeka after the war in Croatia started saying "grandma," and Tamara insisted on the local expression "nona," which is commonly used in the Croatian Adriatic region, that comes from Italian *nonna*. (DD)

CLOACA

is this cloaca-coca-cola[203] or did i pull this can out of the sea and leave it on the beach to lie there waiting for someone to pick it up

—don't dream but be awake and carefully watch this textual cliff which fascinates and mesmerizes you in this enchanted world, but this enchanted world desires the newer enchantment just like the Serbian writers who were enchanted by the decasyllabic verse about which Stanislav Vinaver[204] humorously and convincingly wrote around the mid-20th century

> and as this line tore off and ragged out endlessly i will turn to the other side and omit everything which is not good to notice from big too big or small too small a distance in any case don't blame me because i will ignore/*ignorirati* small and great things and will collect everything I own and don't own and leave this suntanning place behind because the pines cast their mighty shadows and we are helpless we could just cut them down as powerful politicians always do because they cannot bear this strength which comes from beyond economic and political power

POLLUTION

---

[203] Reference to the concrete poem, "beba coca cola," by Brazilian poet, essayist and translator Décio Pignatari (1927-2012). (DD)

[204] Stanislav Vinaver (1891-1955) was a Serbian modernist, poet, prolific essayist and translator, of Jewish origin. At the Sorbonne, he studied with Henri Bergson. He criticized the obsession of Serbian poets with the iambic pentameter of folk songs. Among his extraordinary translations are Francis Rabelais, *Gargantua and Pantagruel*, and Lawrence Stern, *The Life and Opinions of Tristram Shandy, Gentlemen.*

MY LOVE OF NARRATIVE IS SATISFIED BY TELEVISION SERIES my love toward the narrative is satisfied by television series my love toward the narrative is satisfied by television series

first character: why would the latin alphabet be our alphabet[205]

second character: television series after 2000 belgradize serbia and belgrade[206] is not serbia

third character: what all could yugonostalgia mean:
    yearning for one's youth
        idealization of socialism and social security
        a critique of the mononationalism of newly established states and their generating of new identifying matrices

fourth character: although we will talk of a yugoslavian[207] and a post-yugoslavian space, we will do it without any yugonostalgia[208]

---

[205] In Serbia there is a cultural clash over whether to use the Latin and Cyrillic letters or only the Cyrillic. (DD)

[206] Belgrade is the capital of the Republic of Serbia. This is a reference to a statement of one Serbian media studies scholar who, during the rule of the Democratic party, criticized a Serbian TV serial production which insisted on dealing only with urban life, calling this belgradization. (DD)

[207] Socialist Federal Republic of Yugoslavia which was destroyed in the 90s wars. (DD)

[208] In public discourses after 2000, many intellectuals who publicly speak or write about Yugoslavian and post-Yugoslavian cultures felt required to distance themselves from accusations of being Yugo-nostalgic, which has negative connotations. (DD)

and instead of a post-yugoslavian space, it is much better to speak of a south slavic space because doing this we throw an ideological veil on that which it is actually about, even though we are all familiar with it

the moment when actress Branka Petrić[209] in the theatrical performance *Born in Ex Yu* directed by Bosnian theater director Dino Mustafić in Yugoslavian dramatic theater [2010] in belgrade starts speaking in albanian and the Belgrade audience applauds
a selected belgrade audience still applauds her, said my friend Bojana Bratić Ivić[210]

[digression: A MANUAL FOR DIRECTORS / *REDATELJE*: with your theatrical performance you must patronize the audience, actors should perform as many gags as possible, they should shout dirty words and make jokes BECAUSE the audience wants to have fun, wants hilarious laughter—this will attract them—*depoliticization* IS actually HYPER-POLITICIZATION

because working people want entertainment/because anti-intellectually oriented middle class wishes to have fun...]

THE CHORUS SINGS:

WE WANT TO HAVE FUN

WE WANT TO HAVE FUN

prose/poetry which is transcription of real conversations, fragments of conversations, ideological positions, full of views and viewpoints, but everything is directed towards denouncement, denunciation or self-censorship

---

[209] Branka Petrić, a Belgrade actress was married to an Albanian Yugoslavian actor, Bekim Fehmiu (1936-2010), who was famous during the socialist time, and even acted in Hollywood productions of the time. (DD)
[210] Bojana Bratić Ivić, translator of Italian women poets into Serbian, and Croatian and Serbian poets into Italian. Lives between Italy, Croatia and Serbia. (DD)

could an artistic space still be a space for the
freedom of expression–[autonomy of art]
could the space of a classroom still be the
space for academic freedom–[university autonomy]—in
which censorship is constantly in progress and even
more deceitful self-censorship

Because the teacher is like a journalist as any other state officer, etc.
member of the society, sensual political **being** or *stvorenje*—
[CREATURE]—who reacts to the dominants dictated by the political
culture—WHO WHAT WHEN AND HOW—but narratives which frame
phenomena dramatically change and in this change the objects of
representation change as well—the mundane phenomena,
phenomena of political actions and discourses

BUT NOW IS THE RIGHT TIME TO ASK WHAT IS THE STATUS OF
THIS TEXT—DOES IT BELONG TO POETRY which what kind and
whose poetry or does it go out of the scope of poetry and who it is
influenced by and borders a nonfiction essay and pOeTry peie—try

Sounding the Rhythm in Poetry[211]

1.

for Darja Pavlič

writing poetry	---	in which language
writing about poetry	---	in which language
translating poetry	---	from which language
translating poetry	---	into what language

reading poetry	---	rhythmically in your voice
		beats (Nina Dragičević)[212]

reading poetry	---	out loud as loudly as possible
performing poetry	---	with the body of poetry
		with the body of the woman poet
		and her voice

where is the beginning
and where is its end

	---	which end
	---	whose end

waves
waves of the weeping willow
and the lazy walk by the Ljubljanica[213]

murmur		
murmur		by the Ljubljanica

writing poetry	---	in which language

---

[211] The poem was written during the conference in Ljubljana dedicated to the relationship between Slovenian and American poetry organized by scholar Darja Pavlič in 2019. The people that Djurić met there are mentioned in it. (DD)

[212] Nina Dragičević, a Slovenian composer, theoretician, prose writer, poet and lesbian activist. In her poems she deals with the rhythm and sound of the language. (DD)

[213] Ljubljanica—river in Ljubljana, the capital city of Slovenia.

writing poetry

reading poetry   ---   in which language
      reading poetry

performing poetry   ---   in which language
      performing poetry

poem like the spring sun
      emerges from the clouds

the moon like the night sky
      emerges from a poem

little sparrows jump up and down   ---   in which language
    in an urban landscape   ---   in which language
    in a city landscape

turn towards poetry
don't turn away from poetry
wave to poetry

men and women
women and men
          with a slow rhythm
          walk along the Ljubljanica

a walk will fall off the table
    in Šalamun's[214] *hiža*[215]

voice strikes
         how to survive
         how to survive (Nina Dragičević)

---

[214] Tomaž Šalamun (1941-2014) was a Slovenian poet who was a leading figure of postwar neo-avant-garde poetry in Central Europe and internationally acclaimed absurdist. His books of Slovenian poetry have been translated into 21 languages, with nine of his 39 books of poetry published in English.

[215] *hiža*—"house" in Slovenian. Šalamunova hiša (Šalamun's House) is a center for poetry in Ljubljana.

desolation
fullness
small sparrow
mommy
gravel
tree
multitude
margin
the middle/ environment
abstraction
šutnju[216]
emptiness
fullness
repetition
voice strikes
voice strikes
abstraction
abstraction
wind
wind
murmur
ptići žvrgolijo[217]
crows caw

first the blackbirds were banished
then the sparrows were banished
only the blackbirds remain

and the cutting of trees
a real pogrom

that's why my voice modulates
the melody of speech changes
the melody of speech wanders aggressively

           and wanders

---

[216] *Šutnja*—Croatian for "silence."

[217] *Ptići žvrgolijo*—"birds sing" in Slovenian. The phrase comes from a poem of Slovenian experimental poet, Ifigenija Zagoričnik (later known as prose writer Ifigenija Simonovič), as well as a phrase from a children's song. (DD)

extend your hand to the poem
extend your hand to *pepa*[218]

wander roam and wander

women poets
women poets
         are taking over
    the field
         the field of poetry

and what's happening to it

poetry is a job
                just like any other

and poetry needs rhythm
         rhythm

poetry of the short   or
poetry of the long   breath

poetry
poetry   that I love

and poetry
poetry   that I don't love

poetry
poetry   that I write

and poetry
poetry   that I don't write

poetry
poetry   that I am thinking

---

[218] The dear one.

and poetry
poetry   that I am not thinking

abstract poetry
abstract poetry
                                       of the short breath

poetry   that   deals   with   itself
                         doesn't   look

                                                       left
                                                       nor right
poetry
poetry   on a bicycle

and poetry
poetry
                              in the car
                              on the bus
                              on the airplane
                              and on the street
                              and at home
                              and in bed
                              and in the bathtub

poetry
poetry   that sings

and poetry
        poetry   that dances
                        and that smiles
                        and which is joyful
                        and which sobs
                        and which spells out words
                        and swallows musical notes

                        and when I am writing/ write it
                        and when I am not writing/ write it

poetry which   I am dreaming

poetry which thinks of itself
and poetry which thinks of me

poetry is cold
poetry is hot

poetry which sits by the Ljubljanica
                and thinks of itself
                in rhythmical terms

2.
              for Iztok Osojnik [219]

While I am waiting for food
                in a Ljubljana sushi bar

I am thinking of the Beat generation
                    of American poets
And the Beat generation as a transnational phenomenon
        = everywhere and always present

        And I ask myself who else
                could you meet
                      in the center of Ljubljana /Suzana Tratnik/[220]

In small cultures there is
                only a mainstream poetry
                    and it absorbs everything in itself

that's why I am speaking
                    of language
                and thinking of language
                and which language
                and why language

---

[219] Iztok Osojnik—a Slovenian poet and comparatist.
[220] Suzana Tratnik—a Slovenian prose writer, translator, lesbian activist and sociologist.

[*tongue-in-cheek*][221]

           being silent about language
           listening to a language
           being quiet in a language
moving toward a language
and running away from a language

towards an abstract language

a language of *otoka*[222]
a language of *otroka*[223]

              towards a sea language
              towards a coastal language
              towards a pier language
              towards a pain of a language
              towards loneliness of a language
              towards a hill of a language
              towards a nightmare language

encompass a language
And let it be swept away by waves
Mud carries it to the beach
              Of discord

Which language
Why language
Where language

              The pulse of language
              The darkness of language
              The freeze of language
              An abstraction of language
              The pain of language

---

[221] Line is written originally in English.

[222] *Otok*—"island" in Croatian.

[223] *Otrok*—"kid" in Slovenian.

Liana of a language
Line of a language
Eel of a language
The freezing of a language
Love of a language
Hatred of a language
Suffering of a language
Mourning of a language

                                        bereaved language
                                    language in mourning

Remembering of a language
Remembering a language

A myriad of languages
One language

                                My language
                                Not-my language
                                My not-a-language

The dawn of language
The dusk of language

Twilight
Dusk
Darkness

                            The minimalism of a language
                            The abstraction of a language
                            The language of the sea
                            The language of compulsion

Language of war
Language of peace
Language of peace making
War of languages (Josip Sever)[224]

---

[224] Josip Sever (1938-1989), Croatian poet and translator, Sinologist and Slavist. He wrote poetry under the influence of Russian Cubo-Futurism. In 1964 in Moscow, thanks to Gennadiy Aygi, Chuvash poet and translator, who wrote in Chuvash and Russian, Sever met Aleksei Kruchyonikh, a Russian experimental poet and theoretician. This refers to Sever's poem,

A language makes peace
                    With itself

A language makes peace
                    With me

What will that language say
What will it say to me
                    What will it whisper to me
                              And which language
                              And which language will it be
                              And why language
                              And how language
                              And where language

Abstract language
Reistic language
Carnal language
Ludistic language (Taras Kermauner)[225]

Language of philosophy in poetry
Language of theory in poetry (language poetry)
Feminist language in poetry
Language of feminist theory in poetry (Rachel Blau DuPlessis)

Where is the border

                              Between languages
                              Or it doesn't exist

Is *pjesma-pjesen*[226] on the border of

"Ballad of the Croatian or Serbian Language" ("Balada o hrvatskom ili srpskom jeziku"), which begins: "And when definitively slaughter really slaughter / each other, Serbian/ and Croatian words, / What will then / remain? / I suppose / fairy language of animals [*nemušti jezik*] / the language of birds, trees / flowers/ and ants/ and ants/ and children's language." (DD)

[225] Taras Kermauner (1930-2008) was a Slovenian literary historian, critic, philosopher, essayist, playwright and translator. He introduced the term reism (Slovenian: reizam) to point to the Slovenian experimental poetry of the 1960s by Marko Pogačnik, Matjaž Hažek, Iztok Geister Plamen and Franci Zagoričnik, as anti-humanistic that put the question of language at the center of poetry practice. (DD)

[226] *pjesma-pjesen*—"poem" in Croatian and Slovenian.

                                        language
                        Or between languages

How many languages in a single
                                        language

                                                        in a single poem

How many languages

How a language crosses borders
                                        Of languages
                        Borders of their limitations

Poetry in all languages

                                                Poetry above
                                                Poetry below

                        Of languages

Poetry of feelings
Or poetry of *sjećanja*[227]
Poetry of reason
Experimental poetry

Poetry that runs
Poetry that dances
Poetry that sneaks around
        WANDERS AND LOITERS
Stealthy
And invisible

Uvijek[228] witty never ever spiritual
And most certainly serious
Merciful
Or ruthless

---

[227] *Sjećanja*—"memories" in Croatian.
[228] *Uvijek*—"always" in Croatian.

Bipolar
Bilingual
Multilingual
Multipolar

Pliable
And resisting

Rhythmical
And without rhythm

Language-city
Language-*utvrda*
Language fortress
Language-*tvrđa*[229]

A tower of cards language
A sandcastle language
A tower of *pjesma*[230] language
A web of meaning language
Retina language

Magic picture language
Cartography language
Alphabet language
Pencil language
Pre-poetry (Vlado Martek)[231]

Language fret
Language key

On a typewriter/*pisaćem stroju*[232]
On a piano

---

[229] Serbian and Croatian words *utvrda, tvrdjava* and *tvrdja* have the same meaning: fortress.

[230] *pjesma*—"poem" in Croatian.

[231] Vlado Martek—see footnote no. 166.

[232] *stroj*—"typewriter" in Croatian.

On a computer/*računalu*[233]

Pika
Točka
Tačka[234]

                        Rumble of a storm
                        Rumble of the sea
                        Nightmare
                        The most comfortable bed
                                      Lie
                                        Truth
                                      And post-truth
                                            Desert

Desert full of sand
Quick sand of poetry

Dead sea of language
Ancient revived language (Amir Or)[235]
Living dead language

A norm of language
Canon of poetry
        Canonical procedures of poetry
        Canonical procedures of poetry

Dead sea – oblivion
Dead sea of oblivion

Party
Cocktail party art (group KôD)[236]
Cocktail party language

---

[233] *računalo*—"computer" in Croatian.

[234] Words in Slovenian, Croatian and Serbian for "period."

[235] Amir Or—Israeli poet, novelist and essayist.

[236] The title of the work of the Novi Sad conceptual group KôD, whose members were Slobodan Tišma, Slavko Bogdanović, Miroslav Mandić and Mirko Radojičić. All of them, except Radojičić, wrote experimental poetry. (DD)

Pleasure in language
Pleasure of language

Fall into language
Language intrusion
Rising from a language
            Rising from the ashes of a language

Phoenix bird of a poem (Josip Sever[237])
Poem the only bird of a language (Robert Duncan)[238]

A blind street of a language
A blind street of a poem

Exit from a language
Entrance into a poem
            (*bijeg*[239] from poetry – Vlado Martek – Darko Šimičić)[240]

In a poem and around a poem—eye of a poem[241]
For a poem and against a poem

3

                                        for Irena Novak Popov[242]

At the *letališće*[243]

---

[237] Josip Sever—see footnote 218. Refers to his long poem, "Song for Phoenix" ("Pjev za Feniksa"). (DD)

[238] Refers to Robert Duncan's poem "An Owl Is An Only Bird of Poetry." (DD)

[239] *bijeg*—"escape" in Croatian.

[240] Darko Šimičić, a Croatian art critic and curator.

[241] In CBSM languages *oko* means "around" and "eye."

[242] Irena Novak Popov is a Slovenist scholar.

[243] *Letališće*—"airport" in Slovenian.

                    How to say to a poem
                              that it is a poem
                    How to say to a poem
                              that it is not one

who is in a *pjesma*[244] (Barbara Korun)[245]
and who is outside of a *pjesma*

who is covered by a *pjesma*
tko[246] vomits a poem
who returns it to us
pjesma nausea
pjesma joy and *pjesma* happiness
                    (*pjesma* garbage)
                    (*pjesma* honey comb) (Jelka Kernev Štrajn)[247]

                    pjesma faced with its own
                                        shadow (Michael Palmer)
                                        with oneself

pjesma shadow
pjesma   dream (Jerome Rothenberg)
pjesma   sled

sjena[248] of a poem
shadow name of *pjesma*
pjesma letališče
poem locomotive
poem handrail
pjesma honeycomb
pjesma drunk *pjeva*[249]
shocked

---

[244] *Pjesma*—"poem" in Croatian.

[245] Barbara Korun is a Slovenian poet.

[246] *Tko*—"who" in Croatian.

[247] Jelka Kernev Štrajn is a Slovenian comparatist, critic and translator.

[248] *sjena*—"shadow" in Croatian.

[249] *pjeva*—"sings" in Croatian.

enthralled
surprised

I could understand it
(Ljubljana's fog)

I could write it
I could *narisati* it[250]
(Ljubljana's fog)

I could touch it and trace it
(Ljubljana's fog)

could I leave it
pjesmu/pjesen in the fog

bijesna[251] *pjesma*

                    full of anger

the poem's anger   vents

                                            on me
                                            on you
                                            on us
                                            on you (pl.)

mi se zdi[252]
                there is a *pesen*
                        mi se zdi
is is

deer in a forest words of a poem
words of a forest like water
        rustle like leaves
        make noise like waves
WAVES OF A *PJESMA*

---

[250] *narisati*—"to draw" in Slovenian and Croatian.

[251] *bijesna*—"mad" in Croatian.

[252] *Mi se zdi*—"it seems to me" in Slovenian.

naked *pjesma*
dressed *pjesma*

poem of dirty hands
chocolate poem
yum yum
chocolat   e in a poem

rhythm rhythm
letališće

          poem at a *letališće*

words leaves
words *lisje*[253]
words lichen

             lichen of words
             lisje of words

in the rhythm
in the roaming

       words
       words

in rhyme

       words run away from rhyme

rhythm
     the strike of a voice
   the voice screeches
    the poem clicks
a herd of words
a flock of words
a herd of
       rhymes dissociate themselves

framed with a frame of words
       with the crispy surface of words

---

[253] *Lisje*—"leaves" in Slovenian.

220

with a convex mirror (Srečko Kosovel)[254]

blackbird on a branch of words

darkness
and nausea
                    Molk[255]
Powerful word (*močnejša*)[256]
And a weak word

Sharp edge of a cliff
                                        Words
        In a *slovarju*[257]

Poems poems
Poems—snowflakes tiny snowflakes
        Snjeguljica Snjegoručka[258]

Poems—snowflakes tiny snowflakes
Fall on us
        Cover us
                                A res[259]

Meanings meanings
Multiplied words
Repeated in
        A blue rhythm
            Of a poem's abyss

---

[254] Srečko Kosovel (1904-1926) was a Slovenian avant-garde poet, who came out of impressionism, expressionism and constructionism.

[255] *Molk*—"silence" in Slovenian.

[256] *Močnejša* in Slovenian means "more powerful, stronger."

[257] *Slovar*—"dictionary" in Slovenian.

[258] *Snjeguljica* – in Croatian and *Snjegoručka* – in Slovenian means "Snow White."

[259] Slovenian for "really."

Slovar, slovar

Sweet dreams

Poem dances

> Dance of life
> Dance of death

Poem flies
And a poem crawls

> Be careful be careful dangerous
> *Pesem*

And a dangerous poet[260]
And an even more dangerous *pesnica*/woman poet/*pjesnikinja*[261]

And whom does she pull by the nose/little nose the nose
> Pulls by the nose (*pepe*)[262] for the little nose

And whom does she make fun of
> And at whom does she laugh   / *smije*   /   *smijulji*[263]

And why poem
And how poem

And in which language
And why in a language

But not in a language of the
> Original

---

[260] Dangerous *pesem* (poem) and dangerous poet—reference to Vlado Martek's works of pre-poetry.

[261] *Pesnica*—in Slovenian and *pjesnikinja* in Croatian—"woman poet."

[262] *Pepa* and plural *pepe*, dear ones, ideolectic expression.

[263] *Smije*—"laugh" in Croatian; *smijulji*—*giggle* in Croatian.

Or *nikgda*[264] because there is no original

Poems are always a translation
        A mediator in the second
            In the third
                In the n-teenth

                      Language

Never in its own
        never in its own

        because a poem is always
                in the language
        in its own language
                      which
            mediates all the others
                      all the other poems
            mediates all the others
                      all other languages

        mirrored
        stripped
        bordered
        unlimited
        irreducible
            never reducible to themselves

Ljubljana March 15, 2019. Belgrade October 3, 2019

---

[264] *Nikgda*—"never" in Slovenian.

Migrants [Bodies-in-Motion][265]

migrant bodies [bodies-in-motion]—
expelled by force from their homes
wars wars killings killings expulsions
demolished cities, scorched ground
barbed wire—
uncertainty
desolation
refugee centers around which barbed wire fences are raised
borders which separate and cannot be crossed
and wires wires raised everywhere around us

a few years ago refugees were around parks—
covered with blankets / *dekama*—under tents in the city park, in mud
then around them barbed wires—refugee centers—camps—refugee
                                                                camps

with no compassion

migrant men-migrant women are dangerous *others*—move around like
viruses—run away from them—

but the ill bodies of migrant men and women remain invisible—
the drama remains hidden

danger lurks
you can beat them without impunity, abuse them
you can kill them
you can banish them back to the war and the ruins
into starvation into the torched ground—who needs it and what for
the bodies in motion towards a better life
to new imaginary lives which smile
at anyone who wishes to leave

---

[265] The poem was written at the request of Croatian poet, Lana Derkač, who is editing an international anthology dedicated to the migrants, titled *Wire* [*Žica*] to be published by the Croatian Pen Center. (DD)

leave—yes—but the price is high—
they drown—are robbed—objectified they endure abuse—
physical violence
mental abuse
every abuse
at every moment

on the run from desolation in which armies clash and at any moment ALL
dies
houses die plants die animals die water dies rocks scattered into dust
and where does one find peace and where does one find a better country
planting trees for every new life
going to work
going to work on a farm
going into oblivion into the fun of everyday nonsense
small joys
small tenderness
how does carelessness disappear, melt on the ice
of glaciers
where a polar bear in search of a shelter remains without a habitat

and plastic in the sea
and garbage
garbage
garbage
with which we are inundating the planet

endangered species
disappear

forests on fire
migrant men and women are on the move
from continent to continent
bodies-in-motion

running away from robbery
from murders
destruction

and covid-19 mocks them with its sinister laughter
in the unhygienic temporary shelters
but no one says that the migrant body
is susceptible to illness

no one pays attention
everywhere around us barbed wires are raised

hysterical indifference

Note: This poem was written in January 2022. At this moment [March, 2022]
we are witnessing yet another war in Europe with Ukrainians who are running
away from the Russian invasion.

Interview with Dubravka Djurić by Biljana D.Obradović

BDO: What were your earliest poetic influences? Whom did you read?

DDJ: The early influences were Anglo-Saxon imagism, poets from Vojvodina connected with Vojvodina conceptual art, for example Miroslav Mandić at the very beginning and later Vladimir Kopicl and Slobodan Tišma. Kopicl and Tišma's early work remained a constant influence. Then early poetry by Slovenian poet Tomaž Šalamun, who was also in early days connected with conceptual art—he was a member of the famous Slovenian and Yugoslavian OHO group that was influential in Vojvodina and later in Belgrade's conceptual Group 143. Then the Beat poets, who were the most influential US poetry group in Yugoslavia during the 1970s, especially in the 1980s onwards. Also, haiku poetry.

T.S. Eliot was important—we worked a lot on his work in the courses at the Department of General Literature and Literary Theory at the Faculty of Philology. From the 1950s he was the most influential and most translated poet in Yugoslavia. His work helped Yugoslavian poets after the Second World War and after a short period of socialist realism to reestablish modernist poetry production in the context of Yugoslavian socialism. I liked his selected essays which were published at the beginning of the 1960s in translation. In 1988 I even translated two of his essays for a Belgrade literary newspaper, *Književna reč.*

BDO: Were there any other things like art or people that influenced your views?

DDJ: In 1979 I got in touch with the members of the Belgrade conceptual Group 134. I met them in Slovenia in Šempas in Marko and Marika Pogačnik's home. Marko was an important member of the conceptual OHO group and til the war in Yugoslavia began he was frequently a guest in Belgrade giving lectures and having exhibitions. Conceptual art and its textuality were so important. My sensibility for minimalism and linguistic purism in poetry comes from there: first of all the textuality and work of Belgrade Group 143 whose member was my husband, Miško Šuvaković, and through them my focus went towards the Slovenian OHO group and Vojvodina's conceptualism. There is another person from that time who was important, the art historian Biljana Tomić, who in the gallery of now legendary Student Cultural

227

Centre gathered people and she is the one who initiated Group 143. She is a great concrete poet, acting as critic-at-work. As a member of Group 143, she also had an important artistic production (which unfortunately remained invisible).

BDO: Have you always written experimental poetry?

DDJ: I suppose so. But because of this the fact was that my poetry was almost always outside of what critics in Yugoslavia (first of all in socialist Serbia and socialist Croatia) felt is a good poem or good poetry. At the beginning it caused frustration – it was almost impossible for me to publish in magazines. The first time a large number of my poems were published was in the Croatian magazine *Pitanja*, whose editor was the late Hrvoje Pejaković, a critic and poet. And unexpectedly in 1989, I published my first book in the prestigious Edition First book of Matica srpska. The Editor in Chief was the critic and poet, Vasa Pavković.

BDO: Looking back, can you let us know how you think your poetry writing has changed through the years? Tell us about your process.

DDJ: My problem was that I constantly lack the poetry context to work in. So the translation of American poetry which I started in 1983 was an important working reference for my own poetry. And I started writing criticism which was a way to make my male colleagues pay attention to my own poetry. From the end of the 1980s, I connected my work to my translation practice.

Looking back, I could outline the path of my poetry, starting with imagism and haiku. During the socialist time, the spirituality which came with counterculture was important, like Zen Buddhism and Anthroposophy. In the 1980s the discovery of Rudolf Steiner and Anthroposophy which was influential in Belgrade and Zagreb between two world wars was an exotic fascination in the context of late socialism. After a short period of going deep into the discourse of anthroposophy, I returned to poetry. The influence of Russian Cubo-Futurism came through working on Russian Formalism in my college classes and through a Zagreb poet of my generation, Sanja Marčetić. Marčetić was a part of Zagreb *Quorum*, which had a cult status as a multidisciplinary magazine and was very exclusively postmodern. The Editor in Chief was the poet Branko Čegec. From the end of the 1980s, I intensely read another poet from Zagreb, Josip Sever, who met Aleksei Kruchenykh (1885-1968), in the USSR at the beginning of the 1960s.

I intensively read the textual practices of Group 143 and the influence of this was evident. With Miško Šuvaković and our friend Zoran Belić Weiss (who has lived in the US since the second part of the 1980s), we organized work of the informal artistic and theoretical group Community of Space Research (Zajednica za istraživanje prostora). It is a forgotten art formation with a complex artistic and theoretical practice. One of the things that was important for our work was the relation of art and theory, and art and textuality (and implicitly poetry). All this impacted me so deeply. In 1988, I started translating Language poets, and my poetry is written in relation to their practice. The poetry that I wrote in the second part of the 1980s was influenced by these sources: avant-garde poetics and conceptual art textuality, along with Language writing.

With the beginning of the wars in Yugoslavia, I wrote an anti-war book *Traps* (*Klopke*). I was dealing with patterns of Yugoslavian folklore's literary heritage—it was the first and the last time I used rhyme. It was the time of strong anti-modernism in Serbian poetry and this book fits in this milieu. But the poems in this book led me to oral interpretation of my own poems, and the most important moment for this was the visit to Belgrade and Novi Sad by the American Language poets James Sherry and Charles Bernstein in 1991. Here, I must stress that in my own culture there was a powerful poet and artist who experimented with voice and sound poetry—Katalin Ladik, who belonged to Vojvodina's avant-garde. But my own culture didn't provide me with her work as a model for my own practice, instead I came to this poetic practice through Language poetry. In 1992 she moved to Budapest and now is an internationally recognized artist.

After that, we spent a month in the US thanks to Charles Bernstein—at Buffalo SUNY. It was a great and important time for me and for Miško. We also spent some time in New York thanks to the kindness of James Sherry, Deborah Thomas and Charles and Susan Bee. We visited Los Angeles, San Francisco, etc. and met so many poets, especially Language poets that I have translated—all of this was a crucial experience.

BDO: You've worked with many young writers throughout your career and helped establish them as writers and critics. Tell us about them and those who have made great progress that you feel proud of.

DDJ: Actually, I worked with AWIN's[266] group, and it was a special time in Serbia. In 1994, I became a co-founding co-editor of the magazine, *Pro-Femina,* which was connected with Belgrade's antiwar context. I was a lecturer at Belgrade's Center for Women's Studies, which was an educational feminist antiwar NGO. In the 1990s poetry production in Serbia was not interesting at all; most poets wrote in an old, antimodernist fashion dealing with religious and national roots. In *ProFemina* we wanted modern, urban and experimental work. At one moment around 1995, a few younger women poets appeared: Snežana Žabić, who was a refugee from Vukovar, Croatia, and who studied Czech language and literature (now living in the US); Natalija Marković, who studied Russian; Ksenija Simić, who studied mathematics (now also living in the US), with new, different, fresh poetic material, and I invited them to work together. Many poets came later, like Ana Seferović, who left us soon after, (now she lives in Great Britain), who studied the Turkish language; Danica Pavlović, who studied Library Science; Tamara Šuškić, who studied the Italian language; Snežana Roksandić, who worked as a hairdresser and the most important were Ljiljana Jovanović and Jelena Savić (a Roma), who both studied andragogy. Most of us were of mixed Yugoslavian origins. Jovanović and Savić insisted that we should work diligently and seriously—which further enabled us to work more intensely and on a regular basis. At first, these younger poets learned from me, and at some point, we entered the intensive, creative and intellectual interaction. We functioned like a group, and the model was Yugoslavian radical art groups, like Gorgona in Croatia, OHO group in Slovenia, or Group 143 or earlier Vojvodina's conceptualist groups, or the Community for Space Research.

BDO: You've been teaching at a university for a long time now. Tell us about your teaching, research and service (as editor, for example), and how has involvement in these affected you.

DDJ: I started teaching at the Faculty of Media and Communication in 2007, and it was at first difficult—I changed the area of study from literature to media studies and popular culture. It took me time to learn and progress. Working

---

[266] In 1996. I initiate the AWIN School of poetry and theory, gathering younger poets to work together. Sonja Drljević (1942- 2017) was a feminist activist who invited me to work with this group at Belgrade Center for Women's Studies. When the center split into two, we worked at Asocijacija za ženske inicijative (Association for Women's Initiative—AWIN), from this NGO came the name of the group.

with young people is challenging and interesting—I like the job. But at one point, I returned to poetry.

As for editing, in the 1980s I was an editor in the magazine, *Mentalni prostor,* with Miško Šuvaković and our close friend at the time, artist and performer, Zoran Belić Weiss. It was a magazine in which the informal group of artists, who called themselves Community for Space Research, implemented certain cultural politics. This artistic-theoretical community, like many other things I mention in this conversation, are *impossible histories*— formations whose existence has always gone unnoticed in Serbia. In our magazine, we published texts from artists from Yugoslavia and from abroad. It also functioned as a place to collect our working materials, to write a new theory in art (theory written by artists—the special interest of Miško Šuvaković and Zoran Belić Weiss), and issue no. 3 was a catalogue of an exhibition that took place in Manak's House, a beautiful space built around 1830, which belongs to the Ethnographic Museum in Belgrade. We worked with a curator, the late Nina Seferović. Theory and art had the same status—and that was something that I internalized as a poet working with artists and theoreticians.

Meanwhile, I wrote literary criticism intensively. In 1993 Ljiljana Djurdjić (a dear supportive friend and poet who switched to writing prose and who died of Covid-19 at the end of 2021), called me to join a team that would establish a new magazine for women's writing and culture, *ProFemina.* Djurdjić suggested the name of the magazine, having in mind Carolyn Kizer's poem of the same title. She met Kizer through Charles Simic when she was in the US in the 80s. So, four of us: Svetlana Slapšak (who lived between Slovenia and Serbia, but mostly in Ljubljana and many other Western countries), Djurdjić, the poet Radmila Lazić and I decided on the magazine's concept and structure. What I brought to the magazine was this: literature (poetry and prose, as well as art) should always be accompanied by a theoretical or critical text. Our position was antinationalistic, antiwar, and we cooperated with other women's and feminist organizations in Serbia and in the former Yugoslavia. As editors we supported women writers locally, and we functioned politically, publishing writers from other parts of Yugoslavia, participating thus in the process of reconciliation. This was the most important thing for us all. But as we all now know this process tragically failed—the situation now is like it was in 1991. And it should be added, now while we are finishing the work on the book for release in summer 2023, it is even worse due to the war in Ukraine. Working on the magazine Djurdjić, Lazić and I also learned about feminism. We helped in articulating the climate in which women writers, especially poets, felt important and had a venue for publishing and exchange.

BDO: Can you give us an exercise that you like to give to upcoming writers?

DDJ: In AWIN group we worked this way: intensively reading the poetics of different poets, discussing the issues of poetics in poets' texts and reading their poetry and from this experience came writing. Sometimes we wrote together and that was really fun and a joyful experience: we read to each other what we wrote and were so supportive of each other, but also critical. The idea was to maximally intellectualize the approach to writing poetry and learn to think about it as opposed to mainstream anti-intellectualism.

   The first who wrote on our work and supported us is an excellent Croatian poet and critic, Darija Žilić who became a dear supportive friend. She recognized this work and made it visible in the post-YU region as well as in Serbia. Her work at that time, when she wrote a lot on Croatian, Serbian, Bosnian and Slovenian poets, with a focus on female poets, was crucial for all of us. But regretfully, I have to say that the work of AWIN group is also forgotten in Serbia.

BDO: How did you get interested in Language Poetry?

DDJ: Thanks to my connection to the Yugoslavian radical art scene (1948-2023), I was interested in experimental poetry. But in the field of poetry in Yugoslavia from the mid-80s it was over for experimentalism. In 1987 in Zemun's translation magazine for world literature called *Pismo* (established and edited by one of the most important Serbian poets, Raša Livada [1948-2007]), David Albahari, a prose writer and translator of American literature, wrote a review of Ron Silliman's anthology *In the American Tree*. I immediately understood that it could be very important for my own work. The other source of information was an issue of *Critical Inquiry* which I found in the library of the Third Program of Radio Belgrade where a Marjorie Perloff text on language poetry was published. In 1988, Miško and I spent some time in the US and I bought Silliman's anthology and Douglas Messerli's anthology *Language Poetries, The L=A=N=G=U=A=G=E Book* edited by Bruce Andrews and Charles Bernstein and Perloff's *The Poetic of Indeterminacy* and *The Dance of the Intellect* and Lee Bartlett's *Talking Poetry*. I immediately started reading and with my not-so-good English translating the material. In 1988 I proposed to Slobodan Blagojević and Hamdija Demirović (life partners and poets, originally from Sarajevo, who at the time lived in Belgrade and were editors of modernist magazine *Delo*, who both are the translators of American poetry), to make an issue dedicated to American Poetics, so that every poet is presented with poetry and poetics, and they agreed, and we made it. I suggested that Charles Olson should be included, and I wrote the sections dedicated to Louis Zukofsky, Robert Duncan, Denise Levertov and language poets, including Bernstein, Ron Silliman, Barrett Watten, Michael Palmer, Rae Armantrout, Clark Coolidge, Hannah Weiner, Bob Perelman. Blagojević and Demirović added other poets like Eliot, Pound, Stevens, Marianne Moore, Hart Crane, e. e. cummings, Allen Ginsberg, etc.

BDO: How did you come in touch with American Language poets like Bernstein and others?

DDJ: At some point, I wrote to Segue Foundation run by James Sherry and got their catalogue. When *Delo* appeared in 1989, I sent it to Charles at the Segue address, and he immediately responded. He gave me the addresses of other poets and I sent them copies as well, and most of them responded. I remembered that Ron was generous sending me a bunch of his books including *Leningrad: American Poets in the Soviet Union* (I translated one chapter that appeared in 1992 in Zemun's *Ruski almanah* run by my colleague, Russian translator, Zorislav Paunković). This Russian-American connection was fascinating to me as a poet from a socialist non-aligned country like Yugoslavia. And on the envelope, Ron wrote in Cyrillic letters KNJIGI in Russian; I was so excited about that! From that time Charles and I started our correspondence. Miško and I became friends with them and with many other poets.

BDO: Why did Bernstein come to Belgrade initially?

DDJ: James and Charles were invited to Vienna to give a poetry reading in the summer of 1991 at the time when the war in Yugoslavia was about to start. Charles wrote that he and James would like to come, so I organized poetry readings in Belgrade's Association of Writers of Serbia with David Albahari and in Novi Sad's Vojvodina Literary Society with Vladimir Kopicl. Charles started to teach at SUNY Buffalo, and I asked him if it would be possible to get some funding to come to Buffalo. This was realized in 1994, when Miško and I spent some time in Buffalo and other US cities. Thanks to Charles and James, we managed to meet so many of the poets that I had translated.

BDO: When did you decide to translate poetry from English into Serbian?

DDJ: I have to correct you: into Serbo-Croatian, it was its official name and I stick to that. The question of language and naming languages is a question of ideology, politics, identification, etc.

I was in the third year of my studies at General Literature and Theory of Literature and my professors for many books said, "This is a bad translation," so I decided to start translating. I had two anthologies of American and two anthologies of English poetry. My English was not good, and I gave up on English and turned to American anthologies. That is how I started dealing with American poetry. But I always had good friends who helped me. I could say that I learned English by translating it. Translation became an obsession for me. The first translations appeared in 1984 in *Znak*, a student magazine at the Faculty of Philology.

BDO: Whose poetry have you translated from English into Serbian?

DDJ: I have to relativize the question of language again. I was translating into Serbo-Croatian. When Yugoslavia disappeared in bloody wars, I started thinking about the political and ideological construction of language. My mother tongue was Serbo-Croatian, and because from 1991 I published in most parts of the former Serbo-Croatian speaking area, I consider that I speak all those new languages; that is my political decision and position.

In the last few years, the books of poetry by Charles, Bob Perelman, Rosmarie Waldrop and Jerome Rothenberg in my translation appeared in Montenegro and not in Serbia. The publisher, OKF from Cetinje town is run by an important Montenegrin poet, Milorad Popović. Regretfully, I have to say that the destiny of this publisher given the recent dramatic political situation there is not bright. Before this, in 1992, I published a book of poetry, *Sun*, by Michael Palmer, a friend and colleague. Poet and critic, Predrag Dojčinović (who left soon for the Netherlands where he still lives), liked my translation of Palmer's poem in *Delo* and suggested that I should translate something for the magazine, *Pismo*. I also translated the Canadian poet, Joe Blades. I usually choose whom to translate, but this was an order from the poet and editor, Simon Simonović.

I really translated a lot. I started in 1984 with Robert Duncan and Denise Levertov. As I already said, spirituality was important for me during the socialist times, and spirituality attracted me to their work. But from 1991 I almost exclusively translated language poets, their poems and their texts. With Kopicl, I co-edited and co-translated the anthology of new American poetry, *New Poetry Order*, which appeared in 2001 in Montenegro in Oktoih publish-

234

ing house. Coincidentally, Oktoih is a Serbian-oriented publisher while OKF is Montenegro-oriented. The first edition of *Postmodern American Poetry: A Norton Anthology* that Paul Hoover edited was important in realizing our own anthology. Hoover was kind enough to send it to me.

James Sherry, Douglas Messerli, Rosmarie Waldrop, Charles Bernstein, Jerome Rothenberg, Juliana Spahr, Michael Palmer, Marjorie Perloff, Paul Hoover, Rachel Blau DuPlessis, Jerome Sala, Lyn Hejinian, Bob Perelman, Barrett Watten, Peter Ganick, Clayton Eshleman and many others, were so kind and keep sending their books so that I really translated a lot.

BDO: How did you get involved in feminism? What works did you read that influenced you?

DDJ: Feminism was around in Yugoslavia from the mid-1970s, but most of us were not aware of it. Although from my first translations of language poets' texts I got some knowledge, especially from Lyn Hejinian's texts. Also, I think in 1990, an editor in the Third Program of Radio Belgrade suggested that I translate several texts by American theoreticians dedicated to feminist aesthetics, and I did. But when the war broke, all cultural spaces in Serbia became hyper-mono-nationalistic and I didn't feel I could fit into it and moved into feminism. In 1991 I met Biljana Dojčinović, at the Faculty of Philology and we later became friends. When we went out from the faculty building, the demonstrations against the government were on the streets. She was part of Belgrade's Center for Women's Studies, and through her I offered a course on feminism and art in 1994. Biljana and another colleague, Jasmina Lukić, were in literature studies, and because of my involvement in the Belgrade art scene, I knew a lot about it. At the same time, I got an invitation from my colleagues to join the *ProFemina* team which was in the process of negotiation with the future publisher, at that time, independent oppositional Radio B92. In these two unofficial institutions I (and all of us) learned feminism in the context of the Yugoslavian war and antiwar engagement. We all did a lot of translations, and in 1993 Biljana published her book on American gynocriticism, which was her master's thesis at the Department of General Literature. I still worked on translating language poets, but I think that I strongly began to connect poetry experimentation to feminism when I started dealing with Rachel Blau DuPlessis' work.

BDO: What are you most proud of in your work as an editor?

DDJ: First, I have to mention our anthology of Serbian poetry *Cat Painters*, which was and still is a unique and huge project, realized thanks to you. And it should be said that we got in touch thanks to Charles Bernstein. Our contact became crucial for both of us and developed over time.

The book that Miško and I coedited for MIT Press in 2003 was crucial. I think of it as one of the first/seminal books in Yugoslavian studies, and it was made possible again through language poets' connections. Jed Rasula connected us with MIT Press editor, Roger Conover. It has been almost twenty years since it came out, and it is only now that the material this book started dealing with has received more serious attention in the West and especially in the US. It should be said that Miško was the only person at the time who could persuade people from different parts of Yugoslavia (first of all Serbia, Croatia and Slovenia) to work together on this book.

The Anthology of American poetry that I did in 2001 with Vladimir Kopicl was important; Kopicl had an idea to collect narrative and non-narrative poetics together in one book. And of course, AWIN's anthology, *Discursive Bodies of Poetry: Poetry and Poetics of the New Generation of Women Poets* (2004) is crucial for reintroducing the poetry experiment not only in Serbia, but in post-Yugoslavian poetry cultures, not having in mind only Beat poets or the New York School, but Language poets and Black Mountain College poets.

Also, from the beginning of the 1990s, I started translating Marjorie Perloff's texts or had them translated. They were important especially for our work in AWIN. Later, I worked for a couple of years on improving all these translations. They appeared as a book in 2017 titled *Učini to novim* (*Make it New*) that I edited. Marjorie was always so kind to keep sending me her new books.

BDO: Tell us about the work with your husband, Miško Šuvaković, and how you have been influenced by him and he by you.

DDJ: I suppose you could think of us as a creative couple. We went through phases when we worked very closely together and phases when we worked separately. But, of course, this work is always in correlation. The concept of the relation between art and theory comes from him and Group 143 (The Yugoslavian genealogy of this concept I have already described previously.) When I think today about my poetry practice, I think it had more to do with art than with Yugoslavian or Serbian poetries.

When Miško started teaching at the Faculty of Music in 1996, and I was in *ProFemina*, our work started evolving relatively separately. I focused on translation, on the work in *ProFemina* and AWIN, and he worked with the group of younger theater and visual artists and theoreticians called Walking Theory (Teorija koja hoda).

It is crucial to mention some facts. During the 1990s Miško managed to persuade Slobodan Tišma to collect his early poems, which appeared in a book *Vrt kao to* (1997) published by Tišma's friend, Miroslav Mandić, in the edition *Ruža lutanja*. Miško wrote an afterward. At that time the important figure in the Novi Sad art scene was minimalist painter, Dragomir Ugren (the only minimalist painter in Serbia), who was the director of the Museum of Contemporary Art of Vojvodina. Ugren and Miško realized many important exhibitions of the time, among which was the exhibition *Grupa KÔD, Grupa (Ǝ i Grupa (Ǝ-KÔD: Retrospektiva*. I mention this because this worked as a broader context in which we worked in AWIN. And Tišma was important in the 1990s and later for us. From time to time, he would come to Belgrade and give talks in AWIN on his art and on his understanding of poetry.

When Miško started working at the Faculty of Media and Communication seven or eight years ago, I joined the Ph.D. program he established there, teaching experimental poetry and art and Yugoslavian experimental art, so the work became again very close, but also quite different.

BDO: How have politics and the war in the 2000s changed you or have they? As someone of mixed ethnic heritage, someone who sees herself as a Serb, has your mixed heritage been a problem since the war or in fact an advantage, and how have you used that to encourage understanding between the warring sides in ex-Yugoslavia? You've corresponded with writers and published the work of writers from all sides.

DDJ: First, I have to say that poetry is a great place where you can discursively construct your identity and experiment with the huge amount material you find. Secondly, after the decomposition of Yugoslavia, many of us raised as Yugoslavians lost our home country. As a reaction to this fact, I resist any identification. It means that as the politics and ideologies of your environment change, you change your position in time. You could accept new power, or you could resist, and I chose to resist.

In socialist Yugoslavia in the 1980s, when I started publishing poetry, translations and criticism, it was an interesting situation as I see it now (other positions and interpretations are possible by other protagonists differently positioned in this field). We have one multiethnic, multilingual, multicultural state, which gave us a context that we took for granted, and we belonged to this much broader context than just our own local/mono-national one. But in an interesting way at the same time, we belonged to our national poetry corpus (Serbian, Slovenian, Croatian, etc.). So, I started writing more or less exclusively about Serbian poets of my generation, trying to position myself in this production. At the very end of the 1980s and especially at the beginning of the 1990s, I started writing about poets from Croatia: it was a political gesture. During the war, Miško and I constantly exchanged books with friends from Croatia, especially with the poet and artist Vlado Martek and art curator, Darko Šimičić, who were always kind enough to obtain books on art and theory for Miško and poetry and literature for me. There were also many magazines and books I could write about. So, the exchange never stopped. On the contrary, it was intensified. *ProFemina* in this process was also important.

After 2000, the exchange became the official part of the post-war process of reconciliation of post-Yugoslavian nations/states. For example, the newly established Serbian Literary Society and the newly established Croatian Writers' Society for more than a decade got the money from their Ministries of Culture for writers' exchange. Writers, especially younger ones from all parts of the former Yugoslavia, started traveling around and reading and writing about each other. Miško and I traveled a lot to Slovenia and Croatia, and I started knowing more and more about their poetries. Then I wanted to know more about Bosnia-Herzegovina's, Montenegro's and Macedonia's poetry (which in socialist time didn't exist for me). In *Sarajevo Notebooks* (*Sarajevske sveske*), established by late Bosnian writer Vojka Smiljanić-Djikić (1932-2016) and a team from all parts of former Yugoslavia, you could read about literature (and art) in all these new countries. At some point, I realized that I wanted to do comparative Yugoslavian and post-Yugoslavian poetry studies and comparative feminist Yugoslavian and post-Yugoslavian studies. There are people who work on Yugoslavian/post-Yugoslavian comparative studies, but they all are dealing exclusively with prose. I started writing on post-Yugoslavian poetries with a special focus on Serbian, Croatian and, thanks to Slovenist Darja Pavlič, Slovenian poetry.

On the other hand, I decided to write in different, as I call them, post-Serbo-Croatian languages. More and more I started mixing Croatian and Serbian and some other post-Yugoslavian languages in my poetry. The important reference for this was prose by Daša Drndić. As a Croatian, she lived in Belgrade, but because she was critical of Milošević's regime, she was forced to leave and moved to Rijeka, Croatia. She retold stories of how she had to learn Croatian and then in her prose writing she liked to "contaminate" Croatian with Serbian words and phrases, which caused negative reactions from the conservative Croatian establishment. With this, I show that my work is between all these poetry cultures. I could mention two other younger poets, like Maja Solar, a refugee from Croatia, who now lives in Novi Sad, who in her poetry uses words or phrases from Croatian. Or I discovered one interesting poet, Nadija Rebronja from Novi Pazar (a town in southern Serbia), who rejects any national or local identification. So, my identity is still mixed, and I carefully work on it on different levels of my writing and reject any national identification, but this is a complex position and not without contradictions. I remember that the most famous post-Yugoslavian prose writer Dubravka Ugrešić after 2000 at Central European University in Budapest said that in the West, she is considered a Croatian writer. But, at the time, her work could not be published in Croatia because of her critical stance toward nationalism in Croatia.

BDO: How has the work of the Serbian Literary Society helped you since it was established and what about writers from the old organization, the Association of Writers of Serbia?

DDJ: The story of the Serbian Literary Society is interesting and last summer (2021), I wrote about it in, "Experimental Poetry in Yugoslavian and Post-Yugoslavian Literary Spaces: Socialism, War Transition and Beyond," thanks to the kind invitation of Paul Bové editor of *Boundary 2* that will appear this year. In short: the old Association supported Milošević's nationalistic politics, so when Milošević's regime fell, the anti-nationalistic wing of this society rebelled. Among the most active in this were two *ProFemina* editors, Radmila Lazić and Ljiljana Djurdjić, which I am proud of. Because of health issues, I didn't participate in these dramatic events. The result of this, in its core, was a political confrontation that resulted in establishing the new, Serbian Literary Society. The new literary society had a writer's colony, Čortanovci, and many writers from the former Yugoslavia as well as from different parts of the world spent some time there. In 2004 the guests included American poets, Juliana Spahr and Bill Luoma. I met Juliana in SUNY Buffalo and we have been in contact since then. She invited me to be a contributor to *Chain* that she and Jena Osman (whom I also met in Buffalo) edited, and I translated some of Juliana's text and poems.

One aspect of the work of these two literary associations was important to me: the exchange of writers between the Serbian Society of Writers and the Croatian Writers Society (which was constituted in a similar way as the Serbian one). Also, writers from Slovenia, Macedonia, Bosnia and

Herzegovina and Montenegro would come. I would go to see them all and it was a political gesture for me and many other people who did the same to come and see them. Most of us felt this as an important, I would say, ritual of symbolic reconciliation at the micro-social level.

BDO: Where do you see women poets today in Serbia? Whom do you see amongst the younger Serbian poets emerging as a future star?

DDJ: The reconfiguration of the field of poetry in Serbia in, maybe the last five or more years, is the same as more or less everywhere. The production is huge and pretty much decentered. It is not possible to have insight into it. If you don't know the poet, you may not have the chance to see the work. Until the last two years, bookshops rarely had books of poetry (and we rarely bought them from the socialist times, we have been used to getting books for free). But recently many small book presses were established, and they are publishing contemporary Serbian poetry, but also poetry from the post-Yugoslavian region and all over the world. Some of them have coffee bookshops where you can buy poetry. At the same time, there is too much poetry and so little criticism. But there is a contemporary canon, and poetry started functioning as a star system. Despite seemingly different modes of writing that co-exist, the narrative mode again has prevailed, and it is, I suppose, globally the case.

I think that Ana Ristović, who now belongs to the middle generation, has the best status as a poet. She is well known and respected in the post-Yugoslavian region as well as beyond it. Recently another poet, Ivana Maksić, appeared whose work I find so interesting. She studied English language and literature in Novi Sad and translates a lot of American poets, but also different theoreticians, like Stuart Hall, Deborah Cook, Theodor Adorno and Michel Foucault, but also poets like Bob Kaufman and this year Robert Creeley. She defines herself as a precariously self-employed cultural worker who supports herself as a translator and English teacher. There are more and more poets, and this is a time when poetry production is finally female-centered… although in poetry hierarchies, male poets still have more prestige compared to female poets. That is why I don't mention male poets.

BDO: What are your current projects—in writing poetry, criticism, translation…?

DDJ: Unfortunately, I don't have time for translation anymore. The good news is that an anthology of experimental American poetry I had planned to do with OKF from Cetinje a long time ago finally will appear late this year; the focus of the anthology is on language poetry, but I also included some of the Conceptual writers and Flarf poets. I have many poems translated by Michael Palmer, Ron Silliman and Rachel Blau DuPlessi and hope they will appear as books one day. The main project for me is to try to historicize the projects I worked on, AWIN school and *ProFemina*. For the last three years, I have worked on a hybrid text between poetry, prose, drama and essay. A portion of it appeared in Zagreb's magazine *Tema* of which the editor is Branko Čegec, and a part of it appeared in the theoretical magazine, *Novi Izraz,* from Sarajevo. Another part will appear in the selected poems that you have been working on for which I am so thankful.

I also hope to finish my third book on American poetry.

Finally, I will say that what we have done together with these selected poems is a kind of *total translation*. The phrase was introduced by Jerome Rothenberg to describe his translations of Native American poetry. I think this book is structured in three parts. The first and most important is the translation of my poetry. Then we added notes which I think is a parallel text whose function is to contextualize the poems. But at the same time, I think that the notes function as an independent text. At the end is an interview which is another approach to contextualize my work.

Fall 2021

Acknowledgments

These poems first appeared in Serbia in Serbian only (unless otherwise noted) in the following books and are used with the author's permission (in order of appearance):

Oblici i obale oblaci i oblici/ Shapes and Shores Clouds and Shapes 1982-1983. (Bilingual, Transl. from Serbian by Dubravka Djurić, with Rajka Nišavić, and Elena Lačok; self-published, 1989).

Priroda meseca/ Priroda žene—Devet metapoema (Nature of the Moon/Nature of the/Woman—Nine Metapoems. (Prva knjiga Matice srpske, 1989).

Књига бројева (Book of Numbers). (Krovovi and Književna Opština Valjeva, 1994).

Клопке/ Klopke (Traps). (KOV, 1995)

All Over (Feministička 94, 1995)

Ka politici nade (Nakon rata) (Towards a Politics of Hope [After the War]). (Orion Art, 2015).

Razmicanje okvira /Kosa crta / Konteksta (Stretching the Frames/Slash/Context) (OrionArt, 1994, 2020), but was written earlier (1988-1991).

Some of these poems also appeared in the US in the following books and journals and are used with the author's and translators' permission (in order of appearance):

Sulfur, no. 29, Fall 1991, pp. 23-24. (Transl. from Serbo-Croatian by Charles Bernstein and Dubravka Djurić: "Disordering")

ProFemina, Special Issue, 1997, pp.133-4. (Transl. from Serbo-Croatian by James Sherry and Dubravka Djurić: "From Traps")

Cosmopolitan Alphabet (Meow Press, 1995)

Chain, issue in 5 different languages, pp. 61-63 "Identiteti" (Written in Serbo-Croatian and English)

Cat Painters: An Anthology of Contemporary Serbian Poetry. Eds. Biljana D. Obradović and Dubravka Djurić. (Dialogos Press, 2016). pp. 237-244. (Transl. by Biljana D. Obradović: "Rain," "[As If Yes Yes]," and "Silence Is the Only Noise Which Threatens")

Persimmon Tree, www.persimmontree.org, Cynthia Hogue, poetry editor. "Poets from Elsewhere," Tina Barr, guest editor, Summer 2021. Online. (Transl. from Serbian by Biljana D. Obradović: "Nostalgia") https://persimmontree.org/summer-2021-2/poets-from-elsewhere/

Atlanta Review. Karen Head, Chief Editor; Biljana D. Obradović and Dubravka Djurić, guest editors, Serbian issue, 2021, pp. 56-58 (Transl. by Biljana D. Obradović: "the rule of emptiness [after the war], 2015")

Borders in Globalization Review. Natasha Sardzovska, poetry editor, Vol. 3, Issue 2
  (Spring & Summer 2022), pp. 94-96 (Transl. from Serbian by Biljana D.
  Obradović: "Border," "The Border of My Body")
  https://journals.uvic.ca/index.php/bigreview/issue/view/1554
Persimmon Tree, www.persimmontree.org, Cynthia Hogue, poetry editor.
  "Poets from Elsewhere," Pit Menousek Pinegar, guest editor, Summer 2023.
  Online. (Transl. from Serbian by Biljana D. Obradović: "Pri Mraku")

Biographical Note of the Author

Dubravka Djurić was born on February 14, 1961, in Dubrovnik (now in Croatia). A poet, critic and Professor at the Faculty for Media and Communication in Belgrade, she received her B.A. and her Master's in General Literature and Theory of Literature from the Faculty of Philology, University of Belgrade, and her Ph.D. in Literary Theory from the Faculty of Philosophy, Novi Sad. Since 2015 she has acted as President of the Serbian Association for Anglo-American Studies. She is involved in cultural theory, media theory, modern and postmodern poetry theory, gender theory and poetic performance. She has published numerous books of criticism and studies of poetry and art. During the eighties, she was a member of the informal theoretically artistic group, A Community for Researching Space, and she participated in editing her magazine *Mental Space*. She was one of the founders and editors of the magazine *ProFemina*. In the Association for Women's Initiative, she started the AŽIN School of Poetry and Theory. Since 2021 she has been a member of the editorial board of the Croatian feminist magazine *Treća*. Her poetry has been translated into English, Polish, Italian, Bulgarian, Macedonian, Slovenian, Albanian and Hungarian. She lives in Belgrade with her husband, Miško Šuvaković.

She co-edited, with Biljana D. Obradović, *Cat Painters: An Anthology of Contemporary Serbian Poetry* (with a preface by Charles Bernstein: Dialogos Press, 2016), which won the Misha Djordjević Award (2019) and a Serbian poetry issue of *Atlanta Review* (2021). In 2022 she received the Andjelka Milić Award from the Section for feminist research and critical theories of masculinity of the Serbian Sociological Society (Sekcija za feministička istraživanja i kritičke studije maskulinizma, Srpskog sociološkog društva) for her lifetime theoretical, poetical and activist engagement.

Her collections of poetry include *Priroda meseca, priroda žene* (Novi Sad: Prva knjiga Matice srpske, 1989), *Oblici i obale, oblaci i olici/ Shapes and Shores, Clouds and Shaper poems 1982-1983* (Belgrade: author edition, 1989), *Knjiga brojeva* (Sremski Karlovci:Krovovi and Valjevo: Književna omladina Valjeva, 1994), *Klopke* (Vršac: KOV, 1995), *All-Over, Izabrane i nove pesme sa esejima koji odredjuju fazu moje poezije od 1996-2004* (Belgrade: Feministička 94, 2004), *Ka politici nade (nakon rata)* (Belgrade: OrionArt, 2015) and a chapbook in the US, *Cosmopolitan Alphabet* (Buffalo: Meow Press, 1995).

Her critical works are *Jezik, poezija, postmodernizam / Language, Poetry, Postmodernism* (Belgrade: Oktoih, 2001), *Govor druge/ Language of the Other* (Belgrade: Rad, 2006), *Poezija teorija rod/ Poetry Theory Gender* (Belgrade: OrionArt, 2009), *Politika poezije/ Politics of Poetry* (Belgrade: AŽIN 2010) and *Diskursi popularne kulture/ Discourses of Popular Culture* (Belgrade: FMK, 2011).

Her other anthologies include, as co-editor with her husband, Miško Šuvaković, in the US, *Impossible Histories—Historical Avant-Gardes, Neo-Avant-Gardes, Post-Avant-Gardes in Yugoslavia 1918-1991* (Boston: MIT Press, 2003, 2006; as co-editor and translator with Vladimir Kopicl, in Montenegro, *Novi pesnički poredak; Antologija novije američke poezije [New Poetry Order: Anthology of New American*

Poetry] (Podgorica: Oktoih, 2001). She has been one of the coeditors and contributors for *A Megaphone*, edited by Juliana Spahr and Stephanie Young, in the US (Oakland: ChainLinks, 2011).

She has published her translations into Serbian of collections of poems by Charles Bernstein (2016), Bob Perelman (2018), Jerome Rothenberg (2018) and Rosmarie Waldrop (2019) in Montenegro and edited and co-translated selected essays by Marjorie Perloff (2017).

Biographical Note of the Translator

Biljana D. Obradović, born on February 25, 1961, in Bitola (now in Northern Macedonia), is a Serbian American poet, critic and translator. She has lived in Yugoslavia, Greece and India besides the US. She has a B.A. in English Language and Literature from the University of Belgrade, Serbia, an M.F.A. in Creative Writing, Poetry from Virginia Commonwealth University in Richmond, VA, and a Ph.D. in English from the University of Nebraska, Lincoln. She has received the Masaryk Academy of Arts Medal for her Artistic Achievements, Prague, Czech Republic. She is the recipient of the Norman C. Francis Award for Excellence in Research for 2015 at Xavier University of Louisiana, New Orleans where she teaches Creative Writing and is a Professor of English.

Her collections of poems include *Le Riche Monde* (1999), *Frozen Embraces* (2001), which won the Rastko Petrović Award, and *Little Disruptions* (2012), only previously published in Serbia, which appeared from WordTech Editions in fall 2022 in the US, that also published her fourth collection, *Incognito* (WordTech Editions, 2017). Her poems also appear in *Three Poets in New Orleans* (2000).

She has also published translations from English into Serbian of John Gery's *American Ghosts: Selected Poems* (1999), the late US Poet Laureate, Stanley Kunitz's, *The Long Boat* (2007), *Fives: Fifty Poems by Serbian and American Poets,* as editor and translator (2002), Ezra Pound's granddaughter, Patrizia de Rachewiltz's *Dear Friends* (2012), Bruce Weigl's *What Saves Us* (2013) and African American, Niyi Osundare's *The Tongue Is a Pink Fire* (2015).

She has also published translations from Serbian into English of Bratislav Milanović's, *Doors in a Meadow (*2011) and Zvonko Karanović's *Sleepwalkers on a Picnic* (Dialogos Press, 2020).

She is the main translator and co-editor with Dubravka Djurić, of *Cat Painters: An Anthology of Contemporary Serbian Poetry* (with a preface by Charles Bernstein: Dialogos Press, 2016) which won the Misha Djordjević Award (2019), and she co-edited with Dubravka Djurić (and again as the main translator) of a Serbian poetry issue of *Atlanta Review* (2021). She has also edited a collection of essays by the late poet, Philip Dacey, entitled *Heavenly Muse: Essays on Poetry* (Lavender Ink, 2020). She reviews books for *World Literature Today* and is Book Reviews Editor for *Serbian Studies*. Her poems have been translated into Serbian, Italian, Arabic, Chinese, Japanese and Korean. She is married to the poet, John Gery, and they have a son, Petar Gery, now a Junior at Hofstra University located on New York's Long Island.

ROOF BOOKS
the best in language since 1976

Recent & Selected Titles

- BAINBRIDGE ISLAND NOTEBOOK by Uche Nduka, 148 pp. $20
- MAMMAL by Richard Loranger, 128 pp. $20
- FOR TRAPPED THINGS by Brian Kim Stefans, 138 pp. $20
- EXCURSIVE by Elizabeth Robinson, 140 pp. $20
- I, BOOMBOX by Robert Glück, 194 pp. $20
- TRUE ACCOUNT OF TALKING TO THE 7 IN SUNNYSIDE
  by Paolo Javier, 192 pp. $20
- THE NIGHT BEFORE THE DAY ON WHICH by Jean Day, 118 pp. $20
- MINE ECLOGUE by Jacob Kahn, 104 pp. $20
- SCISSORWORK by Uche Nduka, 150 pp. $20
- THIEF OF HEARTS by Maxwell Owen Clark, 116 pp. $20
- DOG DAY ECONOMY by Ted Rees, 138 pp. $20
- THE NERVE EPISTLE by Sarah Riggs, 110 pp. $20
- QUANUNDRUM: [i will be your many angled thing]
  by Edwin Torres, 128 pp. $20
- FETAL POSITION by Holly Melgard, 110 pp. $20
- DEATH & DISASTER SERIES by Lonely Christopher, 192 pp. $20
- THE COMBUSTION CYCLE by Will Alexander, 614 pp. $25
- URBAN POETRY FROM CHINA editors Huang Fan and
  James Sherry, translation editor Daniel Tay, 412 pp. $25
- BIONIC COMMUNALITY by Brenda Iijima, 150 pp. $20
- QUEENZENGLISH.MP3: POETRY: POETRY, PHILOSOPHY,
  PERFORMATIVITY, Edited by Kyoo Lee, 176 pp. $20
- UNSOLVED MYSTERIES by Marie Buck, 96 pp. $18.95
- I AM, AM I TO TRUST THE JOY THAT JOY IS NO MORE OR

Roof Books are distributed by
SMALL PRESS DISTRIBUTION
1341 Seventh Street • Berkeley, CA. 94710-1403.
spdbooks.org

Roof Books are published by
Segue Foundation
300 Bowery #2 • New York, NY 10012
seguefoundation.com